D1645480

All things give God glory

A Catholic Anthology

Yes, you love all that exists, you hold nothing of
what you have made in abhorence
You spare all things because all things are yours,
Lord, lover of life,
You whose imperishable spirit is in all

THE BOOK OF WISDOM (11.22—12.2)

I no longer desire a better world because
I think of creation as a whole; ...
I have come to see that the higher things
are better than the lower, but that the
sum of creation is better than the higher things alone.

ST AUGUSTINE
Confessions, Book 4

All things give God glory

A Catholic Anthology

burns & oates

Burns & Oates

The Tower Building   15 East 26th Street
11 York Road   New York
London SE1 7NX   NY 10010

www.continuumbooks.com

First published 2005

British Library Cataloguing-in-Publication Data
A catalogue record for this book is available from the British Library.

ISBN 0–86012–415–0

Designed and typeset by Benn Linfield
Printed and bound in Great Britain by MPG Books Ltd, Cornwall

CONTENTS

CONTENTS

— CONTENTS —

RACISM

WAR

— CONTENTS —

CONTENTS

—— CONTENTS ——

THE CHILD

— CONTENTS —

— CONTENTS —

— CONTENTS —

CONTENTS

XXI

ACKNOWLEDGEMENTS

I should like to thank the following people for their heroic efforts to see this book through. First my sister Sophie Lawrence, for her unfailing patience and encouragement with the technicalities of the work, Sandra Andrews in Chippenham for her cheerful help and hard work, Sue Cope for her kind patience with the manuscript, Jane Trimm for the use of her computer when mine collapsed, and finally special thanks to Barrie David, who rescued my work so many times without complaint.

The following extracts are used with kind permission of;

A. P. Watt on behalf of the Royal Literary Fund for permission to include The Donkey, by G. K. Chesterton, from The Wild Knight and other poems.

The Telegraph Group for permssion to use 'By Nature an Atheist' by Martyn Harris, May 1996

The Telegraph Group for permission to use the article Infanticide, 25th January, 2004

The C. S. Lewis Company for permission to use Christian Behaviour by C. S. Lewis Copyright C. S. Lewis Pte. Ltd. 1943. Surprise by Joy by C. S. Lewis copyright C. S. Lewis Pte. Ltd. 1955. Letters to Malcolm by C. S. Lewis. copyright C. S. Lewis Pte. Ltd. 1955. The Problem with Pain by C. S. Lewis, copyright C. S. Lewis, Pte. Ltd. 1955. US rights belong to Harcourt Brace

Solo Syndication for use of the article The Baby with a Cleft Palate by Allison Pearson from the *Evening Standard*, 5th March 2004

Dent and Co. for the extract from Quite Early One Morning out of the Collected Stories by Dylan Thomas

FOREWORD

Sally Rena describes herself, in assembling this collection of texts, as being like a caretaker of a block of flats with an amazing sets of tenants. I think of her more as the hostess of the most tremendous party to which she has invited her extraordinary friends. My cousin Sally comes from a family which delights in parties and conversation, and when I was a child she dazzled me with her wit. The fascination of this party is that it brings together people from different faiths and none, and from centuries that are far apart. Part of the pleasure of this book is therefore the juxtaposition of different views, which stimulate one to new thoughts of one's own. It is good to find Homer between St Ambrose of Milan and François Mauriac, or Hilaire Belloc between Napoleon and John Updike, and wonder what sort of conversation they would have had.

It is described as a 'Catholic Anthology'. Most of the authors are Catholics, but a large number are not. It includes texts by members of other denominations, such as C. S. Lewis, of other faiths, and by atheists, such as Bertrand Russell. This is what makes it truly Catholic, open to the breadth of human and religious insight. Catholic is a term that both identifies the members of a Church but is also a challenge to us to learn about God from anyone who has wisdom to offer, for nothing human is alien to Christ.

At first sight it is surprising to find doctrinal texts taken from the Catechism beside poems and meditations. One might imagine that doctrine and poetry are like oil and water, incompatible genres. But Sally Rena is surely right, since true doctrine is never narrow and doctrinaire. It is always an invitation to journey towards the wide open spaces of God's mystery. Anyway who is drawn to that mystery will inevitably need poetry to articulate their intuitions of that which is beyond words. Most of the greatest theologians, such as Augustine of Hippo and Thomas Aquinas, were also poets. Doctrine can point in the right direction, but it is poetry that helps one to travel.

This is not a book to read from cover to cover but to have by one. Sally Rena explains that many of the texts encouraged her when she lost a boy at birth, and they will encourage us too, whatever dramas we may live through. It is a book to which we may turn if we feel puzzled or in need of quotation, or just have a few moments to fill.

I found that this anthology communicates a deep sense of the creativity and resilience of human beings. We are made in the image of the Creator, and every human being has their own spark of creativity. We live in dark times, in the shadow of suicide bombings, war, starvation and the threat of ecological disaster. It has been asserted that Western culture is living through a collective depression. But this collection of texts give one hope, because God's surprising grace is at work, in those who call God by different names, and even those who do not believe in God at all. Humanity will not be finally defeated, and so let us not be cast down now.

TIMOTHY RADCLIFFE OP

INTRODUCTION

I should have liked to call this small book 'Things which have interested me' after an essay by Arnold Bennet. But this would bring me into the foreground where I don't want to be. I feel strongly that this is not my work. I am not an author here. I feel more like a caretaker in a block of flats who has an astonishing collection of tenants to look after.

I must say what this book aims to do. Once I lost a little boy at birth. I thought I should never get over him. The men and women who did the most to help me were not my family or friends, though they did the very best they could. The people who stopped me sinking into despair were the men and women whose work I have collected in this book. Most of them died many centuries ago, but I never feel that when reading their work or their letters. I think of them in the present tense. They are down to earth, bracing in their advice and almost always light-hearted. They have given me help through many difficult times and still do. I feel enormous grati-tude to them. I long for other people to read them and to see just how relevant their words are to the world in which we live today.

I have also included many things in this book which it isn't necessary to know but which are beautiful, such as D. H. Lawrence's poem 'Pax' or the opening lines of Bertrand Russell's *Autobiography*. This brings me to the next point. Many of the excerpts quoted here are written by people who didn't believe in God, or didn't hold with organized religion. But these people too have turned a wise eye on the human condition. They are concerned with their fellow men and, in their poetry, with the beauty and mystery of the world. In this sense they are entirely spiritual.

The articles of doctrine are taken from the Catechism of the Catholic Church, and the little red catechism of Christian doctrine which used to cost a penny. I wanted to know what the Catholic Church had to say on a number of subjects. I think there is now a widespread feeling among us that we don't really need to know 'all these theological rules and regulations' in order to be good. At the same time as this attitude becomes more prevalent, Catholics are often questioned rigorously about their beliefs (at least I am): and it would be good to know what these beliefs are, even if they are defended as badly as I defend mine.

Flannery O'Connor, that great and original voice in American literature, said that the Catholic Church was made up of people who were good, bad and mediocre, but that as Catholics, they accepted the teaching of the Church. I have put here a few of the things we are asked to accept. These are mostly to do with the subjects that either concern people now, such as human cloning or euthanasia, or with others which we may have forgotten about or never even knew, such as the doctrine of Hell or the rules for fasting and abstinence. There are definitions of prayer, conscience and sin, and these by philosophers or saints who have not all been read by all of us.

The mixture is one of facts, doctrine, prayers, meditations and quotations from pieces of poetry which I have collected in a commonplace book for over 40 years. There is also an index of authors at the back of the book. This has thumbnail lives in it – some of them longer than the work quoted, because I've found these indices so useful in other books, or enjoyed them anyway. I've left out entries on such disparate people as Roosevelt and Napoleon out of fear of the obvious!

Finally this is meant to be a book that you dip into, because this way of reading, which is quite like magazine reading, comes naturally to most people. I hope, as I have said, that it may be a help in moments of doubt or low spirits. But mainly I hope this small book is an encouragement to read more of the great men and women who are quoted here.

PRAISE AND THANKSGIVING

God is so great that all things give Him glory
if you mean they should. So then, my brethren, live.

GERARD MANLEY HOPKINS
from *The Principle or Foundation*

I place before my inward eyes myself with all that I am – my
body, soul, and all my powers – and gather round me all the
creatures which God ever created in heaven, on earth, and in
all the elements, each one severally with its name, whether
birds of the air, beasts of the forest, fishes of the water, leaves
and grass of the earth, or the innumerable sand of the sea. And
then the loving arms of my soul stretch out and extend themselves towards the innumerable multitude of all creatures and
my intention is, just as a free and merry leader of a choir stirs
up the singers of his company, even so to turn them all to
good account by inciting them to sing joyously, and offer up
their hearts to God. *Sursum corda.*

BLESSED HEINRICH SUSO
Meditation

Your whole creation is never silent, and never ceases to praise you. The spirit of every man utters its praise in words directed to you; animals and material bodies praise you through the mouth of those who meditate upon them, so that our souls may rise out of their weariness towards you, first supporting themselves upon the things you created, and then passing on to you yourself, who made them marvellously. And there is refreshment and strength.

ST AUGUSTINE
The Confessions

Only to man Thou hast made known thy wayes,
Of all the creatures both in sea and land.
And put the pen alone into his hand,
And made him secretarie of Thy praise.

GEORGE HERBERT
The Temple

Pied beauty

Glory be to God for dappled things –
    For skies of couple-colour as a brinded cow:
For rose-moles all in stipple upon trout that swim:
Fresh-firecoal chestnut-falls; finch's wings;
    Landscape plotted and pieced – fold, fallow, and plough;
And all trades, their gear and tackle and trim.

All things counter, original, spare, strange;
    Whatever is fickle, freckled (who knows how)
        With swift, slow; sweet, sour; adazzle, dim;
He fathers-forth whose beauty is past change:
    Praise him.

GERARD MANLEY HOPKINS

6

Brahman

There is a light that shines beyond all things on earth, beyond us all, beyond the heavens ... this is the light that shines in our heart.

All the universe is in truth Brahman. He is the beginning and end and life of all. As such in silence let us give unto him adoration.

There is a spirit that is mind and life, light and truth and vast spaces. He enfolds the whole universe and in silence is loving all.

CHANDOGYA UPANISHAD

My God and King

Chorus: Let all the world in ev'ry corner sing,
      My God and King.

Verse: The heav'ns are not too high
      His praises there may grow.

Chorus: Let all the world in ev'ry corner sing,
      My God and King.

Verse : The church with psalms must shout
      No doore can keep them out:
      But above all, the heart
      Must bear the longest Part.

Chorus: Let all the world in ev'ry corner sing,
      My God and King.

GEORGE HERBERT

Thanksgiving to God for my House

Lord Thou hast given me a cell
    wherein to dwell:
A little house whose humble roof
    is weatherproof
Under the sparres of which I lie
    Both soft and drie;
Where thou my chamber for to ward
    Hast set a guard
Of harmlesse thoughts to watch and keep
    Me while I sleep,
Low is my porch, as is my fate,
    Both void of state;
And yet the threshold of my doore
    Is worn by the poor
Who thither come, and freely get
    Good words or meat
Like as my parlour, so my hall
    And kitchen small;
A little butterie, and therein
    A little byn
Which keeps my little loaf of bread
    Unchipt, unflead;
Some brittle sticks of thorne or briar
    Make me a fire,
Close by whose living coal I sit
    And glow like it.
Lord I confesse too, when I dine,
    The pulse is Thine,

And all those other bits that bee
    There placed by Thee:
The worts, the purslain, and the messe
    of watercress,
Which out of Thy kindnesse Thou hast sent;
    And my content
Makes those and my beloved beet
    To be more sweet
'Tis Thou that crown'st my glittering hearth
    With guiltless mirth;
And giv'st me wassaile bowls to drink
    Spiced to the brink.
Lord, 'tis Thy plenty dropping hand
    That soiles my land
And giv'st me for my bushell sowne
    Twice ten for one;
Thou mak'st my teeming hen to lay
    Her egg each day,
Besides my healthful ewes to bear
    Me twins each yeare;
The while the conduits of my kine
    Run cream for wine,
All these and better Thou dost send
    Me to this end,
That I should render, for my part,
    A thankfull heart.
Which fir'd with incense, I resigne
    As wholly Thine;
But the acceptance, that must be
    My Christ, by Thee.

ROBERT HERRICK

9

No thanks for little things

Only he who gives thanks for little things receives the big things. We prevent God from giving us the great spiritual gifts He has in store for us because we do not give thanks for daily gifts. We think we ought not to be satisfied with the small measure of spiritual knowledge, that we must be looking forward for the highest good. Then we deplore the fact that we lack the deep certainty, the strong faith, the rich experience that God has given to others, and we consider this lament pious … but how can God entrust great things to one who will not thankfully receive from Him the little things.

DIETRICH BONHOEFFER
Life Together

Cheery Beggar

Beyond Magdalen and by the Bridge, on a place called there
the Plain,
    In summer, in a burst of summertime
    Following falls and falls of rain,
When the air was sweet-and-sour of the flown fine flower of
Those goldnails and their gaylinks that hang along a lime;

    The motion of that man's heart is fine.
    Whom want could not make pine, pine.
That struggling should not sear him, a gift should cheer him,
Like that poor pence of mine, poor pence of mine.

GERARD MANLEY HOPKINS
(unfinished poem)

The Magnificat

My soul doth magnify the Lord,
My spirit doth rejoice in God my Saviour.
For He hath looked on His servant in her lowliness
Henceforth all generations shall call me blessed.

The Almighty hath worked marvels for me.
And holy is His name,
His mercy is from age to age on them that fear Him.

He hath put forth His arm in strength
And scattered the proud-hearted.
He hath cast the mighty from their thrones
And has raised the lowly.

He hath filled the hungry with good things to eat,
And the rich He hath sent empty away.
He protects Israel His servant,
Remembering His mercy,
The mercy promised to our fathers,
To Abraham and his sons forever.

LUKE 1.46—56

O most high, almighty, god

O most high almighty, good Lord God, to Thee
belong praise, glory, honour and all blessing.

Praised be my Lord God with all his creatures,
and especially our brother the sun, who brings us the day
and who brings us the light; fair is he and shines
with a great splendour; O Lord, he signifies unto us, Thee.

Praised be my Lord for our sister the moon and for the stars,
which he has set clear and lovely in the heaven.

Praised be my Lord for our sister water, who is
very serviceable unto us and humble and precious and clean.

Praised be my Lord for our brother fire,
through whom Thou givest us light in the darkness;
and he is bright and pleasant and very mighty and strong.

Praised be my Lord for our mother the earth,
she which doth sustain us and keep us, and bringeth forth
divers fruit, and flowers of many colours and grass,

Praised be my Lord for all those who pardon one another
for his love's sake, and who endure weakness and tribulation;
blessed are they who peaceably shall endure,
for Thou, O most highest, shalt give them a crown.

Praised be my Lord for our sister the death of the body.
Blessed are they who are found walking by Thy most holy will.

Praise ye and bless ye the Lord, and give thanks unto him and
serve him with great humility.

ST FRANCIS OF ASSISI
Trans. unknown

Shadows and shine art Thou

Shadow and shine art Thou,
   Dear Lord to me;
Pillar of cloud and fire
I follow Thee,
Although the way is long,
In Thee my heart is strong,
Thou art my joy my song,
Praise, praise to Thee.

EMILY DICKINSON

Lift up your hearts

Priest: Lift up your hearts
Congregation: We lift them up to the Lord
Priest: Let us give thanks to the Lord our God
Congregation: For it is right to give him thanks and praise.

JUBILATION

The songs of Africa

And so men who sing like this in the harvest, at the grape picking, in any task that totally absorbs them, may begin by showing their contentment in songs with words, but they soon become filled with such happiness, that they can no longer express it in words, and leaving aside syllables, strike up a wordless chant of jubilation.

ST AUGUSTINE
The City of God

The soldiers who came back from the war in Africa in 1945 brought with them recordings of songs which were sung nearly two thousand years after Augustine by men working in the Congo and in Senegal, and these songs were filled with the same unchanging jubilation.

The joy of poetry was, and is the celebration of man which is also the celebration of God.

DYLAN THOMAS

Poems of Felicity

An eager thirst, a burning ardent fire,
A virgin infant flame.
A love with which into the world I came,
An inward hidden heavenly love,
Which in my soul did work and move,
And ever, ever, me inflamed
With restless longing; heavenly avarice
That never could be satisfied.
That did incessantly a paradise
Unknown suggest, and something undescried
Discern, and bear me to it, be
Thy name forever prized by me.

THOMAS TRAHERNE

What makes for human happiness

1. Good health
2. Appreciation of beauty in art and nature
3. A reasonable standard of living
4. Satisfactory work
5. A philosophy to deal with life's vicissitudes
6. A happy marriage

CARL JUNG
General Practice Notebook

Complete happiness

Complete happiness does not exist here. Happiness is a real thing, good and great: but it has its proper region. Christ came from that region of happiness; even He could not find it here.

ST AUGUSTINE
Peter Brown, Augustine of Hippo

THE HEART

The lowest trees have tops, the ant her gall,
The fly her spleen, the little spark his heat,
The slender hairs cast shadows, though but small,
And bees have stings, though they be not great.
Seas have their source, and so do small springs,
And love is love, in beggars and in kings.
Where waters smoothest run, there deepest are the fords,
The dial stirs though none perceive it move;
The firmest faith is found in fewest words,
The turtles do not sing, and yet they love,
True hearts have ears, and eyes, no tongues to speak,
They hear and see and sigh; and then they break.

EDWARD DYER

The False Heart
I said to heart 'How goes it?' Heart replied:
'Right as a Ribstone Pippin' but it lied.

HILAIRE BELLOC

Thou gavest them their heart's desires,
And sent leanness withal into their souls.

PSALM 106

RELIGION

The worship of God is not a rule of safety – it is an adventure of the spirit, a flight after the unattainable. The death of religion comes with the suppression of the high hope of adventure.

A. N. WHITEHEAD

Salvation under anaesthesia
What made religion interesting in the old days was the risk one took with one's soul. The drama was not belittled by modern theologians with their symbolic Christs and their salvation under anaesthesia.

ISAK DINESEN
Letter to Bjornvig

Religion is the cry of the soul in a soulless world, religion is the opium of the people.

KARL MARX
(Critique of Hegel's Philosophy of Right)

The Catholic Church
It must be in God's hands because, seeing some of the people who have run it, it couldn't possibly have gone on existing without some help from above.

HILAIRE BELLOC

Religion is the vaccine of the imagination

I would rather see the children of a village in the hands of a
man who knows only his catechism, but whose principles are
known to me, than of a half-baked man of learning who has no
foundation for his learning and no fixed ideas. Religion is the
vaccine of the imagination. She preserves it from all absurd
and dangerous feelings ... if you take faith away from the
people you will end up with nothing but highway robbers.

NAPOLEON

Lady Juliet Duff (on the death of Hilaire Belloc's wife):
But your religion must be a comfort to you?
Hilaire Belloc: A Comfort? No such thing, The Faith is
not a drug!

CHRISTOPHER SYKES
Nancy: The Life of Lady Astor

These pathetic ugly churches around us are trying to encourage
us to keep on living. At one time people's energy was so great
that the Church was in a scolding position, a discouraging
position; but in these late feeble times, it is trying to keep
us from keeling over.

JOHN UPDIKE
Newspaper interview

... if one is tired all the time, I do not see how one can accept the Christian religion that is so exhausting and tied up neatly for all eternity with rewards and punishments and plodding (one that too much bears the marks of our humanity with its intolerable urge to boss and intimidate).

STEVIE SMITH
Me Again

2,414 paragraphs in the Church's law-book

Lord, you have established rulers in this world, both temporal and spiritual, and sometimes it seems to me that they have diligently set about patching up all the holes that

Your spirit of freedom had torn in the fences of rules and regulations by His liberating Pentecostal storms.

First there are the 2,414 paragraphs of the Churches law-book. And even these haven't sufficed: how many 'responses' to inquiries have been added to bring joy to the hearts of the jurists? And then there are several thousand liturgical decrees clamouring for our attention ...

Then there are also various 'Official bulletins' in the Kingdom of your Holy Spirit, not to mention countless files, inquiries, replies, reports, decisions, meetings, citations, instructions from every kind of Congregation and Commission. And how resourceful the moralists are at asking tricky questions, until all the pronouncements of all higher authorities are neatly ordered and interpreted. What incredible zeal

Your servants and stewards have shown in Your absence, during the whole period of Your journey into the distant silence of eternity. And yet, according to Your own word, where the Spirit of the Lord is, there is freedom!

I don't mean to accuse them. Lord, these wise and faithful servants whom you have placed over Your household. Rather I must say to their praise that they are usually not vulnerable to the reproach Your Son once made against the Scribes and Pharisees who sat upon the Chair of Moses (Matt 23.4). Unlike those rulers and teachers of old, your modern stewards have imposed heavy burdens not only on others, but on themselves too.

KARL RAHNER
Encounters with Silence

The Old Testament God

Mandelstam was rather frightened of the Old Testament God with His awesome totalitarian power. He used to say (and I later found the same idea in Berdiayev) that, with its doctrine of the Trinity, Christianity had overcome the undivided power of the Jewish God. Undivided power was of course to us something of which we were very afraid.

NADEZHDA MANDELSTAM
Hope against Hope

The Transfiguration

Christ did not enchant men. He demanded that they believe in Him. Except on one occasion. For a brief while, Peter, James, and John were permitted to see Him in His glory. For that brief while they had no need of faith. The vision vanished, and the memory of it did not prevent them from all forsaking Him when He was arrested, or Peter from denying that he had ever known Him.

W. H. AUDEN
A Certain World

The Milky Way farmer

The Godhead, the author, the Milky Way farmer, the first cause, architect, lamplighter, quintessence, the beginning word, the anthropomorphic bowler-out and blackballer, the stuff of all men, scapegoat, martyr, maker, woe-bearer. He, on the top of the hill in heaven, weeps whenever, outside that state of being that is called his country, one of his worlds drops dead, vanishes, shrinks, explodes, murders itself. And when he weeps, light and his tears glide down together, hand in hand.

DYLAN THOMAS
Quite Early One Morning

Despair

I understand finally why the love of God created men responsible for one another and gave them hope as a virtue. Since it made of each of them the ambassador of the same God. In the hands of each of them rested the salvation of all. No man had the right to despair since each was a messenger of a thing greater than himself.

ANTOINE DE SAINT EXUPÉRY

Osip Mandelstam to a would-be suicide: Why do you think you ought to be happy? How do you know what will come afterwards? Life is a gift which nobody should renounce.'

OSIP MANDELSTAM
Nadezhda Mandelstam, Hope against Hope

Whatever the abyss from which it comes, the darkness of pain is here on our sunniest landscape, a blot no government can tackle or science dispel. Our frame of security must find room for sorrow together with cruelty and death; and no welfare state can do more than make us tolerably comfortable while things go tolerably well.

FREYA STARK

Epilepsy

You all, healthy people, can't imagine the happiness which we epileptic people feel during the second before our fit. There are moments, and it is only a matter of five or six seconds, when you feel the presence of the eternal harmony ...
a terrible thing is the frightful clarity with which it manifests itself and the rapture with which it fills you. If this state were to last more than five seconds, the soul could not endure it and would have to disappear.

FYODOR DOSTOIEVSKY

Prayer for those out of their minds

When they are so ill that they can no longer trust their minds, we beseech you, Almighty God. to take away their pain.
Stay close to them, their loneliness is too frightening for them to bear. Rescue them quickly, we pray you, from the terror of disintegration and despair.
Keep away from them those who fail to understand them.
Give them back, sweet friend, their reason and their hope, without these how can they survive?

Help them, we beg you, because they cannot help themselves.
And comfort those who have to watch them,
Who fear they have lost the souls of those they love, together
with their minds.
We make our prayer in the name of Christ your Son, who
suffered the same agony of mind.

ANON.

God cannot want from us what is not possible. When we are
so reduced that we cannot entertain thoughts of faith and love,
God no longer wants His will done by us, He wants it done by
others.

ANON.

Pain is an interesting subject for discussion between people
who are not suffering. Those who do suffer have no time to
discuss it. They have all their work cut out to cope.

ELEANOR HAMILTON KING
The Sermon in the Hospital

Therefore, at every moment we pray that, following Him, we
may depart from our anxiety into His peace.

W. H. AUDEN

Keep me from sinkin' down
Oh Lord,
Oh my Lord,
Oh my good Lord,
Keep me from sinkin' down.

I tell you what I mean to do,
Keep me from sinkin' down,
I mean to go to heaven too:
Keep me from sinkin' down.

ANON.
transcribed by Robert Nathaniel Den

For though I knew His love who followéd
Yet I was sore dread
Lest, having Him, I must have naught beside.

FRANCIS THOMPSON
The Hound of Heaven

The intermittent spirit
I am shocked by a fact which nobody ever mentions: the life of
the spirit is intermittent. It goes from full vision to absolute
blindness. The man who loves his wife, finds sometimes that
there is nothing to this love but worries; the man who loves
certain music, finds sometimes that he gets nothing out of it.

ANTOINE DE SAINT EXUPÉRY
Vol de Nuit

That night the spirit went out of me on the mountain. The weight of the rice [Eric Newby was carrying a heavy sack], coupled with the awful cough which I had to try to repress, broke something in me. It was not physical, it was simply that part of my spirit went out of me, and in the whole of my life since then, it has never been the same again.

ERIC NEWBY
Love and War in the Appenines

He shall deliver thee

For He shall deliver thee from the snares of the hunter
And from noisesome pestilence,
He shall defend thee under His wings, and thou shall be safe
   under his feathers;
His faithfulness and truth shall be thy sword and buckler,

Thou shalt not be afraid of any terror by night:
Nor from the arrow that flieth by day:
Nor the pestilence that walketh in darkness:
Nor the sickness that destroyeth in the noon-day.

A thousand shall fall beside thee and ten thousand at thy right
   hand:
But it shall not come nigh thee,

There shall no evil happen unto thee:
Neither shall any plague come near thy dwelling,
For He shall give His angels charge over thee:
To keep thee in all thy ways.
They shall bear thee in their hands!
Lest thou dash thy foot against a stone.

PSALM 90/91

Prayer, the Church's banquet, Angels' age,
   God's breath in man returning to his birth,
The soul in paraphrase heart in pilgrimage
   The Christian plummet sounding heaven and earth.
Engine against the Almighty, sinners' tower
   Reversed thunder, Christ-side piercing spear.
The six-day's world transposing in an hour,
   A kind of tune, which all things hear and tear,
Softness and peace and joy! and love, and bliss,
Exalted manna, gladness of the best,
   Heaven in ordinary man well drest,
The Milky Way, the bird of Paradise,
   Church bells beyond the stars heard, the soul's blood,
The land of spices; something understood.

GEORGE HERBERT

And with the morn those angel faces smile,
That I have loved long since and lost a while.

CARDINAL NEWMAN
Lead Kindly Light

THE WORD OF GOD

THE FOUR GOSPELS

How would you choose which Gospel to read? If you do not have a favourite in mind, I might offer the following guidelines for choosing.

St Matthew's Gospel

St Matthew's gospel is a magnificent total vision. The vision is from eternity to eternity. Thus it can be a very beautiful choice for someone who needs to see the larger meaning of the day-to-day events in which we tend to get lost.

St Mark's Gospel

The great point of St Mark's Gospel is the humanity of Jesus. The Jesus of Mark is the most human of the four because it was the earliest to be written when the Church's reflection on Jesus' divinity was not yet far advanced. This has great importance today when, after several centuries, we are finally coming to terms again with the humanity of Jesus, with His truly human consciousness, and with the fact that ... He has been tempted in every way we are. So if you find in your life that Jesus tends to be rather remote, so divine that you find it difficult to identify with Him in your own human temptation and suffering, then I would suggest choosing Mark.

St Luke's Gospel
[This] is the gospel of social service and also of women:
women play a much more prominent part here than in the
other gospels. Both the stress on social service and the place of
women in Luke probably owe much to his own background as
a Gentile and as a physician. Luke's is also the gospel of the
Holy Spirit, who plays a prominent role here as well as in
Luke's Acts of the Apostles. Even in the 'Our Father'
Matthew's Jesus is concerned about the bread that lasts forever,
whereas Luke stresses the bread we need today.

St John's Gospel
St John's Gospel is the gospel of contemplation. One of the
great devices of John is what is called his irony. Throughout his
gospel events have a double meaning: they mean one thing to
God and another thing to men and women. This repeated
irony is telling us that contemplation is not seeing extraordinary things, seeing visions and hearing revelations. Rather it is
seeing the ordinary things through the eyes of God.

THOMAS H. GREEN

The Word of God is something alive and active: it cuts like a
double-edged sword but more finely. It can slip through the
place where the soul is divided from the spirit, or the joints
from the marrow: it can judge the secret emotions and
thoughts. No created thing can hide from Him; everything is
uncovered and open to the eyes of the One to whom we must
give an account of ourselves.

ST PAUL TO THE HEBREWS 4.12—13

Lectio Divina

In English, *Lectio Divina* refers to spiritual reading based on sacred Scripture. The Word is not only superficially read by the eyes, but is listened to with the ears and received by the heart. It is absorbed, repeated and meditated upon. It is a Word that descends into the heart and slowly fills it. You can imagine how much peace this exercise produces. It is completely the opposite of that anxious and hectic reading, hearing and dialogue of our cities' pace which makes life so tense and tiresome. This monastic reading sets a pattern for us in our approach to all things: not with the devouring haste of a consumer, but with the calm of one who is receiving a gift. Most important, remember that this lectio is divine. Its object is God's Word: the Scriptures.

Vatican II, in paragraph 6 of *Dei Verbum*, repeatedly teaches that this ancient monastic tradition is something for all Christians to rediscover and put back into the heart and practice of the community; that is by a continuous reading of the Scriptures which sets the entire plan of God before us every day, every week, in well determined cycles.

CARDINAL MONTINI
The Future Pope Paul VI

Reading is the careful study of sacred scripture.
Meditation is the pondering of deeper truth hidden from reason.
Prayer is the focusing of the devout heart towards God, which
   banishes evil and makes way for the good.
Contemplation is the exaltation of the soul, ravished by the
   taste of eternal joy.

GUIGO II
The Ladder of Monks

Reading, meditation, prayer and contemplation are so inextricably linked together and support each other in such a way that the first two are pointless without the latter two and one rarely or never reaches the latter without the former.

What is the use of seeing, by means of meditation, what we ought to do if we are not strengthened by prayer that enables the grace of God? ... What is fruitful meditation? That which causes fervent prayer to flower, which is ordinarily the way to sweetness of contemplation, which only rarely or miraculously comes to us without prayer.

CARTHUSIAN NOVICE CONFERENCES
The Way of Silent Love

Smudgers and blunters

The New English Bible might be good enough – if we had never had King James's and the Revised Version. To smudge, to weaken, to blunt to make pallid every beautiful word and the thought it carries – was this worth 24 years work? With the alterations so trivial, nothing to make even the attempt worthwhile? But let not the Friends of Mediocrity be cast down. For nowadays we do not often have the AV or the RV or Great Cranmer's Prayer Book. The churches and the chapels have chosen the new translations. They think they are better for the times. But nothing that is second best is right.

STEVIE SMITH
Me Again

The weakening of the idea of value

Valéry remarked some years ago that words like virtue, nobility, honour, honesty, generosity have become almost impossible to use, or else they have acquired bastard meanings: language is no longer equipped for legitimately praising a man's character.

It is slightly, but only slightly, better equipped for praising a mind: the very word mind, and the words intelligence, intelligent, and others like them have also become degraded. The fate of words is a touchstone of the progressive weakening of the idea of value.

SIMONE WEIL

Science, Necessity and the Love of God

ANGELS

See that you do not look down on one of these little ones, for I tell you that their angels in heaven always see the face of my Father in heaven.

MATTHEW 18.10

Guardian angels
From infancy to death, human life is surrounded by their watchful care and intercession.

CATECHISM OF THE CATHOLIC CHURCH

Beside each believer stands an angel as protector and shepherd leading him to life.

IBID.

Anti-angel aggression

I went to the Sisters to school for the first six years of my life.
At their hands I developed something the Freudians have not
named – anti-angel aggression I call it. From 6 to 15 years it
was my habit to seclude myself in a locked room every so often
and with a fierce (and evil) face, whirl round in a circle with
my fists knotted socking the angel. This was the guardian angel
with which the Sisters assured us we were all equipped. He
never left you. My dislike of him was poisonous. I'm sure I
even kicked at him and landed on the floor. You couldn't hurt
an angel but I would have been happy to know I had dirtied his
feathers. Anyway the Lord removed this fixation from me by
His Merciful Kindness and I have not been troubled by it since
– I forgot that angels existed until a couple of years ago the
Catholic Worker sent me a card on which was printed a prayer
to St Raphael.

The Letters of Flannery O'Connor, edited by Sally Fitzgerald

Prayer to St Raphael

O Raphael, lead us towards those we are waiting for, those
who are waiting for us: Raphael, angel of happy meeting,
lead us by the hand towards those we are looking for. May
our movements be guided by your light and transfigured
with your joy.

Angel, guide of Tobias, lay the request we now address to you
at the feet of Him on whose unveiled face you are privileged
to gaze. Lonely and tired, crushed by the separations and
sorrows of life, we feel the need of calling you and pleading
for the protection of your wings, so that we may not be as

strangers in the province of joy, all ignorant of the concerns of our country.

Remember the weak, you who are strong, you whose home lies beyond the region of thunder, in a land that is always peaceful, always serene and bright with the resplendent glory of God.

IBID.

Longing for beauty

I have no patience with that spurious strength of character which puts up patiently with the absence of good things. Do we not all long for the future Jerusalem? I cannot refrain from longing: I would be inhuman if I did. Indeed I derive some sweetness from my very lack of self-control; and in this sweet yearning I seek some consolation.

ST AUGUSTINE

The Confessions

Prayer – some definitions

But before all else we must ask ourselves what prayer is. Why not take that very simple definition of Father de Foucauld: 'Prayer is thinking of God by loving Him.'

RENÉ VOILLAUME

Faith and Contemplation

St Thomas is right. The essential prayer is the prayer of petition.

VINCENT MCNABB

The Craft of Prayer

Prayer is a means by which the love of God is released into the world.

ANON.

34

Time and Prayer

Whatever time we decide to give to God in prayer, let us give it to him with our thoughts free and disentangled from everything else, resolving never to take this time away from Him again whatsoever toil comes our way.

Let us treat this time as something which no longer belongs to us, and even if you spend this time only aware of your insufficiency, don't let it upset you, even rejoice in it, thinking that you are a very good subject for God's mercy.

ST FRANCIS DE SALES
Letters of Spiritual Direction

Don't imagine that if you had a great deal of time you would spend more of it in prayer. Get rid of that idea! Again and again God gives more in a moment than in a longer period of time, for His actions are not measured by time at all.

ST TERESA OF AVILA
The Way of Devotion

'Our' Time

We try, when we wake, to lay the new day at God's feet: before shaving it becomes 'our' time and God's share in it is felt as a tribute which we must pay out of our own pocket, a deduction from the time which ought, we feel, to be our own.

C. S. LEWIS
Christian Behaviour

Each individual should be able to find perhaps no more than five minutes to be alone with God. It may have to be done outside the home, on the bus, walking to the shops, during a tea break. What matters is the planning of just five minutes in twenty-four hours, given over to being alone with God. Is that so impossible?

CARDINAL HUME
To Be a Pilgrim

Older people and those who have retired from work, or those whose children have now grown up, should, as they grow older, learn once again the elementary rules of prayer, or practise with greater ease what in busier times was not possible.

IBID.

If we intend to give the allotted time to being with God and do not deliberately withdraw that intention, then no matter how it seems to us, we can be sure that God lovingly works within us.

RUTH BURROWS
Living in Mystery

My prayer is that your love for one another will increase more and more and never stop improving your knowledge and deepening your perception, so that you can always recognise what is best.

ST PAUL TO THE PHILIPPIANS 1.9—11

THE UNCONDITIONAL
LOVE OF GOD

If anyone comes to me I will never drive him away.

JOHN 6.37–8

Our Lord gives to give. Not to receive. He is content with the
little we can do for Him ... Think always of what you receive,
never of what you give. This is a far better way of entering
into the love of Our Lord and acquiring a boundless
confidence in Him. He is more interesting than you are even
to yourself.

ABBÉ DE TOURVILLE
Letters of Direction

God is on your side

Be bold enough always to believe that God is on your side and
wholly yours, whatever you may think of yourself ... Accustom
yourself to the thought that God loves you with a tenderness, a
generosity and an intimacy which surpasses all your dreams ...
Have the courage to believe that God's action towards you is a
masterpiece of partiality and love. Rest tranquilly in this abiding
conviction.

IBID.

The love that God bears us is, at any moment, the material and substance of our being. God's creative love, which maintains us in existence, is not merely a superabundance of generosity, it is also renunciation.

SIMONE WEIL

Three Essays on the Love of God

For I am persuaded that neither death nor angels nor principalities, nor powers, nor things present, nor things to come, nor heights, nor depths, nor any creature, shalt be able to separate us from the love of God, which is Christ Jesus, Our Lord.

ST PAUL TO THE ROMANS 8.38—9

Love

Love bade me welcome but my soul drew back,
   Guilty of dust and sin,
But quick-eyed love, observing me grow slack
   From my first entrance in,
Drew nearer sweetly questioning if I lacked anything.

'A guest,' I answer'd, 'worthy to be here'
   Love said 'You shall be he.'
'I, the unkind, ungrateful? Ah, my dear,
   I cannot look on Thee.'
Love took my hand and smiling did reply,
   'Who made the eyes but I?'

38

'Truth, Lord, but I have marr'd them, let my shame
   Go where it doth deserve.'
'And know you not,' says Love, 'Who bore the blame?'
   'My dear, then I will serve.'
'You must sit down,' says Love, 'and taste my meat.'
   So I did sit and eat.

GEORGE HERBERT

Mine are the heavens and mine is the earth,
Mine are the people, the righteous are mine and mine are the
   sinners:
The angels are mine and the Mother of God.
And all things are mine,
And God Himself is mine and for me, since Christ *is* mine
And all for me.
What then dost thou seek, my soul?
Thine is all this, and it is all for thee.

ST JOHN OF THE CROSS
Sayings of Light and Love: 26 and 27

Your unconquerable joy
O God, the source of the whole world's gladness and bearer
of its pain, may your unconquerable joy be at the heart of all
our trouble and distress.

ANON.

He has one great infirmity

He, whom you have taken for your spouse, is the perfection of perfections: nevertheless he has one great infirmity, if I may dare say it – He is blind! And there is one thing He does not know – *arithmetic*. If he could see and calculate properly, our sins would surely constrain Him to annihilate us, but instead His love for us makes Him positively blind ... but to produce this blindness and prevent Him from making a simple addition sum you must know how to capture His heart. That is His weak side.

ST THÉRÈSE OF LISIEUX TO HER NOVICES

It is not what you are or what you have been, that God looks on with His merciful eyes, but what you desire to be.

THE CLOUD OF UNKNOWING

God the unsleeping King

As the sun rising in the morning shines into the house if you open the windows, so God, the unsleeping King, will shine in upon a soul which unfolds itself to Him. For God, like the sun above us, is ready to enter within each one of us, if we are open to Him.

ST JOHN OF THE CROSS

The Lord's my shepherd

The Lord's my shepherd,
  I shall not want,
He maketh me down to lie
  In pastures green,
He leadeth me
  The quiet waters by.

Yea, e'en though I walk
  In death's dark vale,
Yet shall I fear no ill,
  For Thou art with me,
And Thy rod and staff
  Me comfort still.

A banquet Thou hast laid for me
  In presence of my foes,
My head Thou hast anointed with oil,
  And my cup overflows.

Goodness and mercy all my life
  Shall surely follow me,
And in God's house forever more
  My dwelling place shall be.

PSALM 23

ENCOURAGEMENT

Once He told me by way of consolation not to worry, and He said this very lovingly – for in this life we could not always be in the same condition. Sometimes I should be fervent, and at other times not; sometimes I should be restless, and at other times, in spite of temptation, I should be tranquil. But I was to hope in Him and not to be afraid.

ST TERESA OF AVILA
E. Alison Peers, The Life of St Teresa of Avila

We must think of our Lord as loving us more than anyone else, upholding us even when we are ready mercilessly to condemn ourselves. That is the ideal of fatherhood, of friendship and of love. When we know our Lord thus we know him well and everything is easy. The terrible God, the angry, exacting, narrow God, has completely disappeared.

ABBÉ DE TOURVILLE
Letters of Direction

You are accepted

Grace strikes us when we are in great pain and restlessness. It strikes us when our distrust for our own being, our indifference, our weakness, our hostility, and our lack of direction and composure have become intolerable to us.

It strikes us when, year after year, the longed-for perfection of life does not appear, when the old compulsions reign within us as they have done for decades, when despair destroys all joy and courage. Sometimes, at that moment a wave of light breaks into our darkness and it is as though a voice were saying: 'You are accepted'.

J. A. T. ROBINSON
Honest to God

The Tenth Revelation

Our Good Lord said most blessedly:
    'See how I have loved you.'
It was as if he was saying, 'My dearest, look at your maker, your endless joy. How can you pray therefore for anything which delights me and I not most gladly give it to you? For my delight is in your holiness and in the endless happiness you share with me.'

JULIAN OF NORWICH
Revelations of Divine Love

'Thou God see'st me.'

GENESIS 16.13

'Now that does not mean,' she said, 'that He's watching you, with all the uncomfortable overtones that particular phrase has. No, what it means is that He cannot take His eyes off you. He is entranced by you, delights in you, loves you and cherishes you as His own flesh and blood.'

ANON.

The Mysteries of the Rosary

THE FIVE JOYFUL MYSTERIES

1. The Annunciation
2. The Visitation
3. The Nativity
4. The Presentation
5. The Finding in the Temple

THE FIVE SORROWFUL MYSTERIES

1. The Agony in the Garden
2. The Scourging at the Pillar
3. The Crowning with Thorns
4. The Carrying of the Cross

THE FIVE GLORIOUS MYSTERIES

1. The Resurrection
2. The Ascension
3. The Descent of the Holy Spirit
4. The Assumption
5. The Coronation of our Lady

THE FIVE LUMINOUS MYSTERIES

1. Jesus' Baptism in the Jordan
2. Jesus' Self-manifestation at the Wedding of Cana
3. Jesus' Proclamation of God with His Call to Conversion
4. The Transfiguration
5. The Institution of the Holy Eucharist

OUR LADY

The Immaculate Conception and the Assumption

Where on earth did you get the idea that the Virgin Mary was conceived sexlessly? You must be confusing this with the Virgin Birth which is not the birth of the Virgin but Christ's birth. The Immaculate Conception means that Mary was preserved free from Original Sin – Original Sin has nothing to do with sex. This is a spiritual doctrine. Her preservation from Original Sin was something God effected in her soul: it had nothing to do with the way she was conceived.

The Assumption means that after her physical death her body was not allowed to remain on earth and corrupt, but was assumed, or, like Christ's body after the Resurrection, was caused by God to come into its transfigured and glorified state. Now neither of these doctrines can be measured with a slide rule. You don't have to think of the Assumption as the artist has to paint it – with the Virgin rising in an invisible elevator into the clouds. We don't know how the Assumption or the Immaculate Conception were brought about, nor is this a matter for science in any way.

The Letters of Flannery O'Connor, edited by Sally Fitzgerald

She was loved by the pious English

Jesus is thought of as the baby of the poor people who received the tributes of a king. His mother was the most beautiful woman in the world – and how many lovely, loving faces of Our Lady we see in the old glass, wall-paintings and statues which survive in England.

JOHN BETJEMAN

The Parish Church in the 15th Century

Of one that is so fair and bright
    Velut maris stella
Brighter than the day is light
    Parens et Puella,
I cry to thee
To turn to me,
Lady, pray thy son for me,
    Tam Puella,
That I may come to thee, Maria.
    Felix Fecundata,
For all the weary thou art rest,
    Mater Honerata.

MEDIEVAL

Sleep and the Mother of God

The business of broken sleep is interesting. But the business of sleep generally is interesting. I once did without it almost all the time for several weeks. I had a high fever and was taking cortisone in big doses, which prevents you sleeping. I was starving to sleep. Since then I have come to think of sleep as metaphorically connected with the Mother of God. Hopkins said she was in the air we breathe, but I have come to realize her most in the gift of going to sleep and as she contained Christ for a time, she seems to contain our life in sleep for a time, so that we are able to wake up in peace.

The Letters of Flannery O'Connor, edited by Sally Fitzgerald

DOGMA

Dogma can in no way limit a limitless God. The person outside the Church attaches a different meaning to it than the person in it. For me a dogma is only a gateway to contemplation and is an instrument of freedom and not of restriction. It preserves mystery for the human mind. Dogma is the guardian of mystery. Doctrines are spiritually significant in ways we cannot fathom. According to St Thomas's prophetic vision is not a matter of seeing clearly but of seeing what is distant, hidden. The Church's vision is prophetic vision; it is always widening the view. The ordinary person does not have prophetic vision but he can accept it on faith.

The Letters of Flannery O'Connor, edited by Sally Fitzgerald

Error and the Church

Christ never said that the Church would be operated in a sinless or intelligent way, but that it would not teach error. This doesn't mean that each and every priest would not teach error but that the whole Church, speaking through the Pope, would not teach error in matters of faith.

IBID.

What do we mean when we say that the Church is infallible?

When we say that the Church is infallible we mean that when speaking as and for the whole Church, because of the guidance of the Holy Spirit, she cannot teach what is contrary to the gospel; that is in matters of faith or of morals she cannot be in error.

HERBERT McCABE

The Teachings of the Catholic Church

How is the infallibility of the Church expressed?

The infallibility of the Church is ordinarily expressed in the common teaching of her bishops and other preachers; on special occasions when an Ecumenical Council has to decide whether some disputed point of doctrine is the common teaching or not; and, occasionally, by the Pope making a similar decision outside a Council but in consultation with the other bishops. Infallible decisions of this kind are extremely rare.

IBID.

Islam: The submerging of the individual

M. thought that this preference for the Muslim world was not accidental – the people of our time were less suited to Christianity with its doctrine of free will and the inherent value of the person than to Islam with its determinism, the submerging of the individual in the army of the faithful, and the formalized design of an architecture which made man insignificant.

NADEZHDA MANDELSTAM

Hope against Hope

O unholy audacity!

We contradict the Lord to His face when we say, 'It is hard, it is difficult; we cannot, we are men; we are encompassed with frail flesh.' O blind madness! O unholy audacity! We charge the God of Knowledge with a two-fold ignorance; that He does not seem to know what He has made nor what He has commanded, as though, forgetting the human weakness of which He Himself is the author, He imposed laws upon man which He cannot endure.

PELAGIUS

THE WILL OF GOD

Simone Weil said she had questioned herself on the will of
God and on the way one could manage to conform to it:

1. By external necessity, that of events which do not depend
   on us.

2. By duty, which concerns personal things and which is
   ordinarily clear and manifest.

3. Through the inspirations which God sends us. God rewards
   the soul which thinks of Him with love and attention,
   by exercising a compulsion upon it.

SIMONE PETREMENT

Simone Weil

God's will to be done by us and to us

There are, according to St Francis de Sales, two arms to the
will of God.
1. God's will to be done.
2. The will of God's good pleasure or God's will done to us.
In the first place there are many things which I am not obliged
to do either by the Commandments or by the duties of my
own vocation. With these it is necessary to consider carefully,
in liberty of spirit, what would tend to the greatest glory of

God, because that is what God wills, and in liberty of spirit because this should be done without pressure or anxiety, but by a simple glance at the good which our action can produce – such as, for example, to visit a sick person, to give a small sum of money for the love of God.

If it is not a matter of great importance then we mustn't invest a great concern in it … and if it looks like I have made a mistake, I should in no way blame myself.

ST FRANCIS DE SALES
Letters of Spiritual Direction

God's good pleasure
This phrase is taken by St Francis from Matthew 2:25: 'I praise you, Father, Lord of heaven and earth, because you have hidden these things from the wise and learned and revealed them to little children. Yes Father, for this was your good pleasure'.

There are matters about which there is no doubt whether God wills them, such as trials, illnesses and chronic conditions. That is why we must accept them with a good heart and conform our will to that of God who permits them.

But we must go further and see this will not only in great affairs but even in little reversals and minor inconveniences that we shall always have to meet with in this unhappy life. In this regard many people make a mistake because they prepare themselves only for major afflictions and remain totally without defence, strength or resistance when it comes to small ones. Actually, it would be more understandable to be prepared for the little ones which come up every day and at every moment.

IBID.

Belief in false gods

To believe in God is not a decision we can make. All we can
do is to decide not to give our love to false gods. In the first
place we can decide not to believe that the future contains
an all-sufficient good. The future is made of the same stuff
as the present.

We are well aware that the good we possess at present, in
the form of wealth, power. consideration of friends, the love
of those we love, and so on, is not sufficient: yet we believe
that on the day we get a little more we shall be satisfied.
We believe this because we lie to ourselves. If we really
reflect for a moment we know it is false.

Or again, if we are suffering illness, poverty, or misfortune,
we think we shall be satisfied on the day when it ceases. But
there too, we know it is false. So soon as one has got used to
not suffering one wants something else.

In the second place we can decide not to confuse the
necessary with the good. There are a number of things we
believe to be necessary for our life. We are often wrong,
because we should survive if we lost them. But even if we
are right, even if there are things which would destroy our
vital energy, that does not make then good: because nobody
is satisfied for long with purely and simply living. One always
wants something more. And we should become miserable with
not knowing what to want. A thing everybody can do is to
keep his attention fixed upon this truth.

SIMONE WEIL

Three Essays on the Love of God

It is infinitely difficult to renounce even a very slight pleasure or to expose oneself to a very slight pain for the sake of God, the true God who is in heaven and nowhere else. Because to make an effort is to approach, not towards suffering, but towards the death of the thing within us which says 'I'.

IBID.

The death of the self
The self is not annihilated by committing suicide but by accepting the good in everything that depends on us and by accepting necessity in everything that does not.

IBID.

DAILY LIFE

God is close to us

Brother Lawrence spoke to me, openly and with deep fervour, of his way of going to God. We need only realize that God is close to us to turn to Him at every moment, to ask for His help, to learn His will in doubtful things, and to do gladly those things we see He requires of us, offering them to Him before we begin, and giving Him thanks when they have been finished for His honour.

That our sanctification does not depend upon certain works, but in doing for God what we would ordinarily do for ourselves.

That he (Brother Lawrence) found the best way of reaching God was through those ordinary occupations which (as far as he was concerned) he received under obedience: doing them for the love of God and with as little regard for human respect as possible.

That we ought not to get tired of doing little things for the love of God, because He looks at the love rather than the work.

BROTHER LAWRENCE
The Practice of the Presence of God

The Sacrament of the present moment

To leave the past to the mercy of God, the future to his providence, is the kind of excellent advice we would cheerfully prescribe to others. How difficult though to practise it

ourselves! The present moment is the only moment we have.
It is only in the here and now that we meet God.

BISHOP JOHN CROWLEY
Prayer in a Busy Life

The person who has learned to practise the presence of God,
and to be happy alone with Him, has discovered something
more than peace in heaven; he has found peace on earth.

RONALD KNOX

I would not have you go to any mortifications

I will tell you what is the greatest — viz: to do well the ordinary
duties of the day. Determine to rise at a certain hour — to go
through certain devotions — don't oppress yourself with them,
but keep to your rules. You will find it sufficient trial!

CARDINAL NEWMAN
Letter, April 1853

God wants a different thing from each of us, laborious or easy,
conspicuous or quite private, but something which only we
can do and for which we were created.

EVELYN WAUGH
Letters of Evelyn Waugh, edited by Mark Armory

Listening

Many people are looking for an ear that will listen. They do
not find it among Christians because these Christians are
talking when they should be listening. But he who can no

longer listen to his brother will soon no longer be listening
to God either. He will do nothing but prattle in the presence
of God.

DIETRICH BONHOEFFER
Life Together

You never thoroughly intended it

If you will here stop and ask yourselves why you are not as
pious as the primitive Christians, your own hearts will tell you
that it is neither through ignorance nor inability, but purely
because you never thoroughly intended it.

WILLIAM LAW
The Spirit of Prayer

A smooth and easy life

A smooth and easy life, an uninterrupted enjoyment of the
goods of providence, full meals, soft clothes, the feeling of
security, the consciousness of wealth – these and the like, if
we are not careful, choke up all the avenues of the soul
through which the light and breath of heaven come to us.

CARDINAL NEWMAN
Plain and Parochial Sermons

Christ is walking among us

We are slow to master the great truth, that Christ is walking
among us, and by His hand, or eye, or voice, bidding us follow
Him. We do not understand that His call is a thing which takes
place now. We think it took place in the apostles' day but we
do not look out for it in our own case.

IBID.

Lift up your heart to Him even at meals and when you are in
company: the least little remembrance will be acceptable to
him. You need not cry very loud; He is even nearer to us than
we are aware of.

BISHOP JOHN CROWLEY
The Practice of the Presence of God

Experience

I disagree utterly with that modern philosophy which regards
experience as fundamental. Experience is a mere whiff or
rumble, produced by enormously complex and ill-deciphered
causes; and in the other direction, experience is a mere
peephole through which glimpses come down to us of
eternal things.

GEORGE SANTAYANA
Letter to Iris Origo

Our affairs

We ought to act with God in the greatest simplicity, speaking
to Him frankly and plainly, and imploring His assistance in our
affairs just as they happen.

BROTHER LAWRENCE
The Practice of the Presence of God

Progress and improvement

Our Lord doesn't want you to think about your progress or
about improvement in any way whatever; but to receive and
use faithfully the occasions of serving Him and of practising the
virtues at every moment without worrying long reflections,
either on the past or the future.

ST FRANCIS DE SALES
Letters of Direction

Prayer as a duty

What can be done for, or what should be done with, a rose tree that dislikes producing roses?

If we were perfected, prayer would not be a duty, it would be a delight. Some day, please God, it will be. If I loved my neighbour as myself, most of the actions which are now my moral duty would flow out of me as spontaneously as songs from a lark or fragrance from a flower. Why is this not so yet? ... The very activities for which we were created, are, while we are on earth, variously impeded by evil in ourselves or in others. Not to practise them is to abandon our humanity. To practise them spontaneously and delightfully is not yet possible. This situation creates the category of duty, the whole specifically moral realm ...

I must say my prayers today whether I feel devout or not, but that is only as I must learn my grammar if I am to read the poets.

C. S. LEWIS
Letters to Malcolm

Praying in secret

When you pray, go into your room, shut the door and pray to your Father who is unseen. And your Father, who sees what is done in secret, will reward you.

MATTHEW 6.6

Our Saviour is not talking about a room with four walls separating you physically from others, but the room that is within you, where your thoughts are shut up, the place which contains your feelings. This room of prayer is with you at all times, wherever you go it is a secret place, and what happens there is witnessed by God alone.

ST AMBROSE
On Cain and Abel, Bk 1

Centring prayer

How to do it

Centring prayer encourages us to wait in silence upon God. As we do so we empty our minds and imaginations, so that God can fill us with His love. As a help in this self-emptying before God, centring prayer teaches the use of a 'prayer word'. How this works is best described in the following three rules:

1. At the beginning of the prayer we take a minute or two to quieten down, and then move in faith to God dwelling in our depths; and at the end of the prayers we take several minutes to come out, mentally praying the 'Our Father' or some other prayer.
2. After resting for a bit in the centre of a faith-filled love, we take up a single, simple word (Jesus, Love, or something similar) that expresses this response and begin to let it repeat itself within.
3. Whenever in the course of the prayer we become aware of anything else, we simply return to the present by means of this prayer word.

When we pray this way we are not trying to get anything. It is simply time we give to God. It is difficult to say what happens in centring prayer.

We leave the results to God. If He wants us to experience His love for us, fine. If we find we are so distracted that we must use the prayer word continually, that is fine too.

Practical advice

People sometimes ask if centring prayer is for everyone. Well, it may not be for those who are comfortable with other prayer forms: the rosary, meditation, charismatic prayer, or any other prayer approved by the Church. There is a basic rule which is valid for all: 'Pray as you can, and not as you can't.'

While there is no proscribed position for centring prayer it is important to avoid tension and strain. Generally it is best to sit, with the back straight. You should be comfortable and relaxed, able to breathe deeply from the abdomen. (A firm chair which gives good support to the back, thighs and knees, is best for most people).

People who pray when they feel like it make little progress. We can all pray when we feel like it. The test comes when we feel dull and dry and yet keep on praying nonetheless. This is what develops us spiritually. Ten minutes a day, five days a week, faithfully adhered to, is far better than attempting twice that amount seven days a week – and then giving up when we find we have undertaken too much.

JOHN JAY HUGHES
Praying in Silence

Friday Penance

Here is the statement on Penance of the Bishops of England and Wales together with the official view about fish on Friday.

Full text of the Bishops' statement, January 1985

1. The new Code of Canon Law reminds us that *all of Christ's faithful are obliged to do penance.* The obligation arises in imitation of Christ himself and in response to his call. During his life on earth, not least at the beginning of his public ministry, Our Lord undertook voluntary penance.

He invited his followers to do the same. The penance he invited would be a participation in his own suffering, an expression of inner conversion and a form of reparation for sin. It would be a personal sacrifice made out of love of God and our neighbour. It follows that if we are to be true, as Christians, to the spirit of Christ, we must practise some form of penance.

2. *So that all may be united with Christ and with one another in a common practice of penance, the Church sets aside certain penitential days. On these the faithful are to devote themselves in a special way to prayer, self-denial and works of charity.* Such days are not designed to confine or isolate penance but to intensify it in the life of the Christian all through the year.

3. Lent is the traditional season of renewal and repentance in the Church. The New Code reaffirms this. It also prescribes that *ASH WEDNESDAY and GOOD FRIDAY are to be observed as days of fasting and abstinence.* Those over eighteen are bound by the law of fasting until the beginning of their sixtieth year, while all over the age of fourteen are bound by the law of abstinence. Priests and parents are urged to foster the spirit and practice of penance among those too young to be the subjects of either law.

4. Because each Friday recalls the crucifixion of Our Lord, it too is set aside as a special penitential day. The Church does not prescribe, however, that fish must be eaten on Fridays. It never did. Abstinence always means the giving up of meat rather than the eating of fish as a substitute. What the Church does require, according to the New Code, is

that its members abstain on Friday from meat or some
other food or that they perform some alternative work
of penance laid down by the Bishops Conference.

5. In accordance with the mind of the universal Church, the
Bishops of England and Wales remind their people of the
obligation of Friday Penance, and instruct them that it may
be fulfilled in one or more of the following ways;
a) By abstaining from meat or some other food;
b) By abstaining from alcoholic drink, smoking, or some
form of amusement;
c) By making the special effort involved in family prayer,
taking part in the Mass, visiting the Blessed Sacrament or
praying the Stations of the Cross;
d) By fasting from all food for a longer period than usual
and perhaps by giving what is saved in this way to the needy
at home and abroad;
e) By making a special effort to help somebody who is poor,
sick or lonely.

6. The form of Penance we adopt each Friday is a matter of
personal choice and does not have to take the same form every
Friday. Failure to undertake this Penance on a particular
Friday would not constitute a sin. However, Penance is part
of the life of every Christian and the intention to do Penance
on Friday is an obligation. We are confident that the Faithful
of England and Wales will take this obligation to heart in
memory of the Passion and Death of Our Lord.

FAITH

I want to understand something of the truth which my heart
believes and loves. I do not seek thus to understand in order
to believe, but I believe in order to understand.

ST ANSELM
The Proslogian

Prayer is a supreme act of faith for there is nothing whatever
to justify such a 'waste of human time' save faith in the unseen,
unperceived holy mystery.

SISTER RUTH BURROWS
Living in Mystery

Christian Orthodoxy

I write from the standpoint of Christian Orthodoxy. Nothing
is more repulsive to me than the idea of myself setting up a
little universe of my own choosing and propounding a little
immoralistic message. I write with a solid belief in all the
Christian dogmas ... I find that this in no way limits my freedom
as a writer and that it increases rather than decreases my vision.
It is popular to believe that in order to see clearly one must
believe in nothing. This may work well enough if you are
observing cells under a microscope. It will not work if you are
writing fiction. For the fiction writer to believe in nothing is

to see nothing. I don't write to bring anybody a message.
As you know yourself this is not the purpose of a novelist; but
the message I find in the life I see is a moral message.

The Letters of Flannery O'Connor, edited by Sally Fitzgerald

... Faith comes and goes. It rises and falls like the tides of an
invisible ocean. If it is presumptuous to think that faith will
stay with you forever; it is just as presumptuous to think that
unbelief will.

IBID.

I think the reason why so many Catholics are repulsive is that
they don't really have faith but a kind of false certainty. They
operate by the slide rule and the Church for them is not the
body of Christ but the poor man's insurance. It's never hard
for them to believe because they never think about it.

IBID.

Don't most people simply drift away?
Now faith, in the sense I am now using it here, is the art of
holding onto things your reason has once accepted, in spite of
your changing moods. Now that I am a Christian I do have
moods in which the whole thing looks very unlikely: but when
I was an atheist I had moods in which Christianity looked
terribly probable. This rebellion of your moods against your
real self is going to come anyway. That is why Faith is such a
necessary virtue. Consequently one must train the habit of faith.

The first step is to recognize the fact that you *have* moods. The next is to make sure that, if you have accepted Christianity, then some of its main doctrines shall be deliberately held before your mind for some time every day. That is why daily prayers and religious reading and church-going are necessary parts of the Christian life. We have to be continually reminded of what we believe. Neither this belief nor any other will automatically remain alive in the mind. It must be fed. And as a matter of fact, if you examined a hundred people who had lost their faith in Christianity, I wonder how many of them would turn out to have been reasoned out of it by honest argument? Don't most people simply drift away?

C. S. LEWIS
Christian Behaviour

If shadows cross your mind on matters of faith, it is because it is so little taught in relation to our actual needs that we cannot always see our way ... everything has to be remade, even that which does not change in itself. Take Nature, for instance. Has it changed? And yet you see in your chemistry and physics that the manner of knowing it has changed. Methods have improved and the same things are seen more clearly. That is precisely what is needed in matters of faith.

ABBÉ DE TOURVILLE
Letters of Direction

Original sin

Original sin is a kind of necessary flaw in the universe. The story of the Fall is a short way of describing the eternal infidelities of mankind, and we now have to put Adam into the plural because science shows us a humanity plunging into the animal kingdom by a large bundle of roots.

TEILHARD DE CHARDIN
Letter to Lamare, 1922

Christ must be endowed with certain physical properties – 'theandric' as theology puts it – radically different from those of a simple prophet who is a vehicle of truth without being in the least a centre which organizes the universe. Christ must always be far greater than our greatest conceptions of the world, but for two centuries we have allowed him to appear hardly equal to them or even smaller. That is why Christianity is so anaemic at the present moment.

TEILHARD DE CHARDIN
Letter to Valesin, 1926

It is the nature of man to believe and to love: if he has not the right objects for his belief and love he will attach himself to the wrong ones.

BLAISE PASCAL
Pensées

CONVERSION

By nature an atheist, by profession a cynic

Excerpts taken from an article in the Daily Telegraph *by Martyn Harris, who died at 43.*

Eight months ago I wrote an article about having cancer, which ended on quite an optimistic note. After a long course of chemotherapy I seemed to be getting better and I had found out things about myself which I felt gave me some new reasons for living. Since then I have had two relapses, two courses of radiotherapy, and two stem cell transplants. The words I wrote last September seem rather smug in retrospect, but in certain ways I feel calmer and more optimistic than I did then.

I was, I wrote then, the last person who should have got cancer – not just because I was only 42, with three children, and reasonably healthy, and a fine chap all round – but because I had imagined myself getting cancer at least once a day every day of my life. I was a compulsive brooder over minor spots and lumps and also indecently terrified of death … so much so that my only way of dealing with it had become to induce a kind of mental white noise. There were certain poems about death, such as Philip Larkin's 'Aubade' and 'Next, Please', which I found so frightening that for years at a time I could not even read them, however much I admired them. Larkin's bleak vision of 'the total emptiness for ever/The sure extinction that we travel to/And shall be lost in always' seemed as unanswerable as it was intolerable.

Perhaps it is paradoxical, then, that one of the things I kept asking myself when I was very ill last summer was 'Why not kill yourself?' My treatment did not seem to be working, I had no hair, my skin was tissue thin, I had continuous nausea, diarrhoea, blinding headaches, blurred vision – so in many ways it would have been a physical relief. There was also the illogical idea that I could cheat the hangman, evade the furnace glare of the fear of death by pre-empting the whole process, with an overdose of pills or by gassing myself in the car. That would teach Death a lesson.

The best reason I could come up with for not killing myself was that it is always better to keep on keeping on even when life is pointless. The decision to live is, in a way, parallel to the decision most of us make every day to try to be good rather than bad people. In a universe without God or an afterlife, which is what I felt reluctantly obliged to accept, the only imperative to behave well is the knowledge that it is more dignified than to behave badly. It is better to resist entropy. It is better to live than not to live, and in deciding this we make ethical creatures of ourselves. It is just about the only tiny nugget of moral truth that the twentieth century has been able to extract from the wasteland of scientific materialism.

As I say, that was where I stood eight months ago. A philosopher would call it an 'existential' position, and I still think it is good solid ground for a moral atheist. But my own ground, I find, has shifted beneath my feet … As the gossamer stuff of ambition, money and possessions fades away, as it always does in time of crisis, I have more seen more clearly how the real structure of my life is my wife and children, my family and friends; their love for me and mine for them. People I never knew before

have been immensely kind, beyond any call of social duty –
people can speak so directly to each other if they try. The feeling
is that there really is a kind of co-inherence to humanity.

I was brought up in the Methodist church but stopped going
when I was 14 or so, and refused to be confirmed ... As an
arrogant would-be intellectual I wanted to hear arguments
about things which really mattered, such as the existence of
God, the truth of the Resurrection and the problem of evil.
But there wasn't much intellectual meat to be had in chapel:
the ministers never seemed to deal with the basics of belief,
instead making laboured attempts to draw up-to-date parallels
with the Gospel stories. It was as if science and the modern
world had terrorized religion out of tackling its own central
mysteries.

I couldn't help noticing that most of the congregation seemed
to consist of old widowed ladies, and that such young people
as there were always seemed to be the least attractive and most
badly dressed types that one wanted to avoid at school.
I concluded, with the cruel certainty of youth, that religion
was for old people afraid of dying, and for young people who
couldn't pull.

I was never quite an atheist though. The triumphalism of
science (any minute now we'll show you the face of God) seemed
quite as silly as the foam-flecked enthusiasm of fundamentalist
religion. I was set on a literary career and it seemed impossible
to imagine a literature which thrived within the closed systems
implied by a science which promised Ultimate Answers to
Everything.

The core of Christianity, as I'd always understood it, was love.
Not just love your neighbour, but love your enemy. Turn the

other cheek. Suffer the insult not seven times, but seventy seven times. As an impatient and short-tempered person, I'd been very bad at practising it but at least I could see it was a tremendously potent political insight.

From a hamlet in Palestine it conquered the Empire in three centuries and without a battle. In our time, in the form of peaceful resistance, it has displaced the British from India, won the fight for civil rights in the southern USA, overturned apartheid in South Africa, even brought down Communism. For though you could argue that it was economic forces and political manoeuvre and even sporadic violence which helped defeat those regimes, it was ultimately those great pacific crowds of common people, from Delhi to Warsaw to Mississippi to Berlin, which were decisive.

I have been talking so far as if all this pondering took place in a vacuum but in fact I was reading a good deal at the time … especially the New Testament. Although I went to Sunday School until I was about 14, I am ashamed to say I never read a single Gospel all the way through, though they are slender things which you can get through in an hour or two …

Grotesquely, I found I was embarrassed to be seen reading them, and would shuffle the Bible under some other book if anyone came into the room. What would my friends think? Poor old Martyn: the cancer has made him go over to the God squad.

But I found I enjoyed the Gospels; the poetic compression of language; the suggestive and paradoxical thought patterns of the teaching, above all the force and authority of Jesus' personality which comes scorching through all the small faults of repetition and translation and human recollection. No fair-minded person could read through these stories without acknowledging that here at the very least is a phenomenon in history, whose mere acquaintance drove men to sacrifice their homes and families and ultimately their lives to spread the story across the known world in a single generation. Any single summary would be too crude, but here was a story which was saying that the creation is not ultimately accessible to or controllable by human reason, that it is the root cause of our human misery to demand that it must be, that God was willing to die to show us the way out.

... I could go on for quite a time here about my surprise at the intellectual coherence of Christianity: at the feebleness of much of the materialistic position which I had assumed to be so impregnable. But one of the things I have learned while writing this article, which has cost me more than almost anything I have ever written, is that ultimately you cannot argue yourself or anyone else into faith. I have had to spike about 6000 words to find myself giving reluctant assent.

Faith is crucially and essentially nonsensical. It is confirmed, if at all, by the most elusive kind of personal experience of order and comfort, of belonging for which the frissons provided by art or nature or human love are only clumsy metaphors. I believe the experience is there for anyone if you are desperate enough, as I have been, or open enough, or perhaps simple enough, but even the best poets have been able only to sketch around the edges of it. T. S. Eliot in *Four Quartets* talks of 'the unattended/ Moment, the moment in and out of time', George Herbert writes of 'Church bells heard beyond the stars, the soul's blood/ The land of spices. Something understood'.

MARTYN HARRIS
Weekend Telegraph, May 1996

The most reluctant convert in England

You must picture me alone in that room at Magdalene, night after night, feeling whenever my mind lifted even for a second from my work, the steady unrelenting approach of Him whom I had so earnestly desired not to meet. That which I greatly feared had at last come upon me. In the Trinity Term of 1929 I gave in and admitted God was God, and knelt and prayed: perhaps the most dejected and reluctant convert in England. I did not see then what is now the most shining and obvious thing: the Divine humility which will accept a convert even on such terms ... The words *compelle entrare*, compel them to come in, have been so abused by wicked men that we shudder at them, but properly understood, they plumb the depths of the Divine mercy. The hardness of God is kinder than the softness of men, and His compassion is our liberation.

C. S. LEWIS
Surprised by Joy

The deepening of conversion

In the matter of conversion, I think you are thinking about the initial conversion. I am thinking possibly about the deepening of conversion. I don't think of conversion as being once and for all and that's that. I think once the process is begun and continues that you are continually turning towards God and away from your own egocentricity and that you have to see this selfish side of yourself in order to turn away from it.

The Letters of Flannery O'Connor, edited by Sally Fitzgerald

73

Do not do violence to yourself, respect in yourself the oscillations of feeling. They are your life and your nature: one wiser than you ordained them. Do not abandon yourself altogether either to instinct or to will. Instinct is a siren, will is a despot. Be neither the slave of your impulses and sensations of the moment, nor of an abstract and general plan but give your life unity and bring the unforeseen within the lines of your plan. Let what is natural raise itself to the level of the spiritual, and let the spiritual become once more natural.

HENRI-FRÉDÉRIC AMIEL
Journal

Our own perfection

We are not to dream of perfection in the abstract but to try to achieve our own special kind of perfection which depends on our character and our circumstances.

This grand and simple teaching has now been superseded by one which is extreme and exaggerated, a distilled perfection … made up of all that is most exceptional in exceptional characters. This standard is then set for all and we are told there is no other: that there is only one kind of perfection and that it is the same for everybody.

We are the brothers and sisters of the saints. They became holy in their way; we must become holy in ours, not theirs.

ABBÉ DE TOURVILLE
Letters of Direction

I don't mean that we shouldn't head in the direction of
perfection, but that we mustn't try to get there in a day,
that is a mortal day, for such a desire would upset us, and
for no purpose. In order to journey steadily, we must apply
ourselves to doing well the first stretch of the journey, and
not waste time wanting to do the last lap of the way.

Treat as suspect all those desires which, in the common
opinion of wise people, cannot be followed up. Such as would
be, for example, the desire for a certain kind of Christian
perfection that can be imagined but not carried out, one that
many people can talk about but that no one puts into practice.

ST FRANCIS DE SALES
Letters of Spiritual Direction

Turn your eyes from the things which pass.

PLATO

Why so much effort?

It is clear that for the Western nations life is a devouring and
incessant activity ... why so much effort, noise, struggle and
greed?

It is all a mere stunning and deafening of the self. When death
comes we recognize that it is so – why not admit it sooner?
Activity is only beautiful when it is holy – that is to say when
it is spent in the service of that which does not pass away.

HENRI FRÉDÉRIC AMIEL
Journal

MISSIONARIES

Campion's brag
(to the right Honourable, the Lords of Her Majesty's Privy Council)
Clause viii: Many innocent hands are lifted up to heaven for
you daily by those English students, whose posteritie shall
never die, which beyond seas, gathering virtue and sufficient
knowledge for the purpose, are determined never to give you
over but either to win you heaven, or die upon your pikes.

EVELYN WAUGH
Edmund Campion: A Biography

And did those feet in ancient time,
Walk upon England's mountains green?
And was the Holy Lamb of God
On England's pleasant pastures seen?

And did the Countenance Divine
Shine forth upon our clouded hills,
And was Jerusalem builded here
Among those dark satanic mills?

Bring me my bow of burning gold!
Bring me my arrows of desire!
Bring me my spear! O clouds unfold!
Bring me my chariot of fire!

I will not cease from mental fight,
Nor shall my sword sleep in my hand
Til we have built Jerusalem
In England's green and pleasant land.

WILLIAM BLAKE
Milton, Preface

The World Council of Churches – The Barbados Declaration, 1971

Final Declaration:

The Council insisted that the missionaries cease to regard Indian beliefs as pagan and heretical. True *respect* for Indian culture must replace the long shameful history of despotism and intolerance characteristic of missionary work, which rarely manifests sensitivity to aboriginal religious sentiments and values. There was to be an end to the theft of Indian property by religious missionaries who appropriate labour, lands and natural resources as their own, and missionaries were to fight harder against such fraud by others. The Conference condemned Indian boarding schools, such as those run by the Salesians on the Rio Negro. These filled their pupils with alien values and, in the name of evangelization, caused an increase in morbidity, mortality, and family disorganization among Indian communities. Missionaries must stop competing with one another for 'Indian souls'. And they should 'abandon those blackmail procedures implicit in offering goods and services to Indian society in return for total submission'. In fact it would be best if all missionary activity were suspended 'for the good of Indian society and for the moral integrity of the churches involved ...

JOHN HEMMING
Die if You Must

Charles Wagley, American Anthropologist

The Indians could easily have been swallowed up by the expanding frontier, as ranch hands or as miserable loafers in Santa Teresinha. In my opinion, it was the arrival of the Little Sisters of Jesus and of Padre François Jentel and their residence in New Village that saved the Tapirape from total disorganization and, probably, extinction.

Both the padre and the nuns tried to intervene as little as possible in Tapirape life. Never did I hear these missionaries attempt religious proslytism. They hoped to influence 'by living example' and not by persuasion. Several times in the 1960s Padre François travelled to Brasilia, where he lobbied with the SPI (Indian Protection Service) for lands for the Tapirape. The Little Sisters and Padre François were able to persuade the Tapirape to continue their subsistence activities; they sometimes supervised barter transactions with itinerant Brazilian traders who came to the village seeking animal skins and 'Indian' artefacts; they urged the Tapirape to travel to 'see the city'; and above all, they gave them pride in their own customs and ceremonials.

IBID.

A rally of the Chiefs of the Xingu against dams on the Xingu River.

The indigenous nations of the Xingu, together with relatives from many parts of Brazil and the world, affirm that we must respect our mother nature. We urge that the forests and rivers, which are our brothers, should not be destroyed. We decided that we do not want the construction of dams on the Xingu or on other Amazonian rivers, because they threaten indigenous nations and other riverine settlers. For a long time, white men have assaulted our thinking and the spirit of our ancestors. They must now stop. Our territories are sacred sites of our people and the dwelling-place of our creator: they must not be violated.

IBID.

The rally was successful.

The four freedoms
Freedom of speech
Freedom of religion
Freedom from want
Freedom from fear

FRANKLIN D. ROOSEVELT

DOING GOOD

He who would do good must do it in minute particulars: general good is the plea of the scoundrel, hypocrite and flatterer.

WILLIAM BLAKE

Jerusalem

The seven corporal works of mercy

1. To feed the hungry
2. To give drink to the thirsty
3. To clothe the naked
4. To harbour the harbourless
5. To visit the sick
6. To visit the imprisoned
7. To bury the dead

Thus says the Lord:
Share your bread with the hungry,
And shelter the homeless poor,
Clothe the man you see to be naked
And turn not from your own kin.
Then will your light shine like the dawn
And your wound be quickly healed over.
Your integrity will go before you,
And the glory of the Lord behind you.

Cry, and the Lord will answer:
And he will say, 'I am here.'
If you do away with the yoke,
The clenched fist, the wicked word,
If you give your bread to the hungry,
And relief to the oppressed,
Your light will rise in the darkness,
And your shadow becomes like noon.

ISAIAH 58.7—10

Christ has no body now on earth but yours:
   No feet but yours;
   No hands but yours;
Yours are the eyes through which is to look out
   Christ's compassion for the world;
     Yours are the feet
   With which He is to go about
     Doing good;
Yours are the hands with which He is to
     Bless men now.

ST TERESA OF AVILA

Comfort thy careworn, Christ, in thy riches
But beggars about mid-summer go breadless to supper,
And winter is yet worse, for they are wet-shod wanderers,
Frozen and famished and foully challenged,
And berated by rich men so that it is rueful to listen to.
Now Lord, send them summer, or some manner of happiness,

81

After their going hence, for what they have here suffered.
For thou mightest have made us equal, none meaner than another,
With equal wit and wisdom, if such had been thy wishes.
Comfort thy creatures who have such a care to suffer
Through dearth, through drought, all their days here.
Who in winter want for clothing,
Who seldom in summer-time sup fully,
Comfort thy careworn, Christ, in thy riches.

WILLIAM LANGLAND
Piers Plowman, trans. Neville Coghill

A poor man

Master: What sort of man are you?
Poor man: A king.
Master: Where is your kingdom?
Poor man: My soul is my kingdom for I can so rule my senses, inward and outward, that all the desires and powers of my soul are in subjection, and this kingdom is greater than any kingdom on earth.
Master: What brought you to this perfection?
Poor man: My silence, my high thoughts, and my union with God. For I cannot rest in anything less than God. Now 1 have found God: and in God I have eternal rest and peace

MAESTER ECKHART

Do something kind to somebody

My dear

Don't dwell too much upon whatever may be wrong: to some minds it may be necessary, but not to those who are in danger of becoming indolent by too much thinking about themselves: and when you find yourself overpowered as it were by melancholy, the best way is to go out and do something kind to somebody. Objects either rich or poor will generally present themselves in the hour of need to those who look for them in earnest, although Oxford is not perhaps the most convenient place to find them in ... I always reckon it a great privilege of a country parson that his resources in this way lies close at his own door.

JOHN KEBLE
Letters of Spiritual Council

A man, to be greatly good, must imagine intensely and comprehensively; he must put himself in the place of another and of many others; the pains and pleasures of his species must become his own. The great instrument of moral good is the imagination.

PERCY BYSSHE SHELLEY
The Defence of Poetry

Be kind, be kind, and you will be saints.

JAN DE RUSBROEK

We are committed to the poor not because the poor are good but because God is good.

DOM GUSTAVO GUTTIEREZ

A rich widow

A rich widow had built a home for old people at the other end of the town. … I got the impression that little gratitude was felt for this act of benevolence, even that there existed a certain resentment against such people who belied the general reputation of their kind for being screws and misers.
For is not generosity too a luxury?

GERALD BRENNAN

The Face of Spain

Sei tu ricco, si? Or sappi che tu sei spenditori di Dio.
So you're rich, are you? Know then that you are God's almoner.

SAN BERNARDINO OF SIENA

The poor and Samuel Johnson

He loved the poor as I never yet saw anyone else do, with an earnest desire to make them happy. 'What signifies' says someone, 'giving halfpence to common beggars? They only lay it out in gin and tobacco.' 'And why' says Johnson, 'should they be denied such sweeteners of their existence? It is surely very savage to refuse them every possible avenue to pleasure, reckoned too coarse for our own acceptance. Life is a pill

84

which none of us can bear to swallow without gilding; yet
for the poor we delight in stripping it still barer, and are not
ashamed to show even visible displeasure, if ever the bitter
taste is taken from their mouths.' In consequence of these
principles he nursed whole nests of people in his house, where
the lame, the blind, the sick and the sorrowful found a sure retreat
from all the evils whence his little income could secure them.

PIOZZI'S ANECDOTES

When you sit happy in your own fair house,
Remember all poor men who are abroad,
That Christ, who gave this roof, prepare for thee
Eternal dwelling in the house of God.

ALCUIN OF YORK
Trans. Helen Waddell

Racial prejudice

... racial prejudice offended her most of all. Regarding the
Africans as subhumans, they required their field hands to
work through the daily rainstorms, and their Somali servants
to interrupt their prayers. When Tanne (Isak Dinesen) tried to
discuss the differences between the races as if there might be
some basis for comparison, the English ladies laughed at her
'originality'. White moral superiority, she concluded, was an
illusion, and by all important standards – honour, for example,
or humour – the Africans were far more civilized.

JUDITH THURMAN
The Life of a Storyteller: Isak Dinesen

The Black People of the Southern United States

Nearly sixteen millions of hands will aid you in pulling the load upward, or they will pull against you. We shall constitute one third and more of the ignorance and crime of the south, or one third of its intelligence and progress; we shall contribute one third to the business and industrial prosperity of the South, or we shall prove a veritable body of death, stagnating, depressing the body politic.

BOOKER T. WASHINGTON
Up from Slavery, 1895

I will let no man drag me down so far as to hate him.

IBID.

The seven capital sins and their opposite virtues

1. Pride	1. Humility
2. Covetousness	2. Liberality
3. Lust	3. Chastity
4. Anger	4. Meekness
5. Gluttony	5. Temperance
6. Envy	6. Brotherly love
7. Sloth	7. Diligence

Mean second thoughts

If one sees a man struggling in the bottom of a well, one's
natural impulse is to pull him out. If a man is starving, one's
natural inclination is to share one's food with him. Surely it is
only on second thoughts that we don't do these things? Society
seems to me to be like an organized system of rather mean
second thoughts.

L. H. MYERS
The Pool of Vishnu

Ingratitude

On my road to Calvary I have seen dozens, even hundreds of
super-educated Marxists, dyed-in-the-wool orthodox communists,
who in their terror-stricken moments turned toward Him whose
existence they had so authoritatively denied for so many years
and in so many talks and lectures. But those who managed to
survive addressed their thanks not to God, but at best, to
Nikita Kruschev. Or to no one at all. Such is our nature.

EVGENIA GINSBERG
Within the Whirlwind

WAR

The Just War Doctrine
The conditions for legitimate defence by military force:
1. The damage inflicted on the nation or community of nations must be lasting, grave and certain.
2. All other means of putting an end to it must have been shown to be impractical or ineffective.
3. There must be a serious prospect of success.
4. The use of arms must not produce evils and disorders graver than the evil to be eliminated. The power of modern means of destruction weighs very heavily in evaluating this condition.

Catechism of the Catholic Church

On a plaque in Senlis Cathedral, Picardy
To the 100,000,000 men of the British Empire who died in France

In the summer of 1914 when he had less than five months to live — he was killed aged 26, a week before the Armistice — Wilfred Owen wrote to Osbert Sitwell:
For fourteen hours yesterday I was at work — teaching Christ to lift his cross by numbers and how to adjust his crown: and not to imagine his thirst until after the last halt. I attended his supper to see that there were no complaints; and inspected

his feet to see that they were worthy of the nails. I see to it that he is dumb and stands to attention before his accusers, with a piece of silver I buy him every day, and with maps I make him acquainted with Golgotha.

WILFRED OWEN

The modern language of war

May 1st

Today I read a xerox of Herman Kahn's article on 'Escalation' from a recent issue of *Fortune*. It is fantastic. His peculiar vocabulary gives it a bizarre, comic quality. But this is not funny, far from it ... since Kahn is so close to speaking the mind of Pentagon officials.

The dispassionate, 'scientific' lingo of games-theory war! At no point does Kahn suggest that the megadeaths he plays with might involve people. Mass murder is simply a language, a means of bargaining, the vernacular of military wheeler-dealing. You evacuate a city. You take out two of the enemies' cities.

And of course the game gets very interesting: 'slow motion counter property war' 'constrained force reduction salvo' 'slow motion counter city war', in which the game takes on something of the allure of a striptease, a tantalizing way to divest the map, bit by bit, of its population. 'City trading.' It is a true 'test of nerves' too, he reminds us. He wants to sell us his toy.

THOMAS MERTON
A Vow of Conversation

Sardinian prayer in 1940

Ave Maria, gratia plena,
Fa' che non suoni la sirena,
Fa' che non vengano gli aeroplani,
Fa' che si dorma fino a domani.

Se qualche bomba cade giú,
Gesu, Guiseppe, Maria,
Fate che gli Inglesi perdano la via,
Dolce cuore del mio Gesu,
Fa' che gli Inglese non vengano piú.

Hail Mary, full of grace,
Grant that the siren doesn't sound,
Grant that the airoplanes don't come,
Grant us to sleep until tomorrow.

Holy Mother think of us,
Jesus, Joseph and Mary,
Grant that the English lose their way,
Sweet heart of Jesus,
Grant that the English never come again.

IRIS ORIGO
War in Val D'Orcia

A definition of peace

Peace is the tranquility of order, created by just political communities, and mediated through law.

ST AUGUSTINE
The City of God

SCIENCE, ETHICS AND RELIGION

In your studies and scientific research rest assured that no contradiction is possible between the certain truths of faith and established scientific facts. Nature, no less than revelation, proceeds from God, and God cannot contradict Himself.

Do not be dismayed even if you hear the contrary affirmed insistently, even though research may have to wait for centuries to find the solution of the apparent opposition between science and faith.

POPE PIUS XII
To the students of the Sorbonne, 1949

Freud on religion

Religion is an attempt to get control over the sensory world in which we are placed, by means of the wish world which we have developed within, as a result of biological and pyschological necessities. But it cannot achieve its end (as defined by Freud). Its doctrines carry within them the stamp of the times in which they originated, the ignorant childhood days of the human race. Experience teaches us that the world is not a nursery. The ethical commands to which religion seeks to lend its weight require some other foundation, since human society cannot do without them, and it is dangerous to link up obedience to them with religious belief.

SIGMUND FREUD
Ernest Jones, The Life and Works of Sigmund Freud

No 'new ethical commands' replaced those which Freud wished to see superceded. And even while he was writing the above in 1938 a deadly ethical vacuum was in the making which allowed the theories described below to be put into action, and which led eventually to the bombing of Nagasaki and Hiroshima.

Bombing the civilian population

The fascist theory of total warfare was first put forward by the Italian General Douhet ... The believers in this theory held that wars could be won by unlimited aerial attack upon the civil population. The demolition of Warsaw and the centre of Rotterdam brought this theory into action. Instead of recoiling against it and concentrating our whole might on the fighting area, we imitated our enemies. By the practice of obliteration bombing (alias strategic bombing) we lost any edge of moral superiority we originally held over the enemy. This general moral disintegration paved the way for the use of the atomic bomb.

Lewis Mumford on the Condor Legion, 1945

The mystery of Majorana

Ettore Majorana was 32 in 1938 when he disappeared after buying a ticket for the Naples to Palermo ferry. It was presumed by the police that he had killed himself, though his body was never found. Majorana's family never considered he was dead and neither did Leonardo Scia Scia, the great Sicilian writer. Scia Scia wrote the Mystery of Majorana *because he became convinced that Majorana, at the time of his supposed death, had entered a Carthusian monastery in Sicily and that the monks had always protected his anonimity. Majorana's loss to science caused great public interest because he was already a major figure in Italian physics at a time when the Nobel Laureate Enrico Fermi and other great scientists were still working there.*

Fermi said of Majorana after his disappearance:
Because you see, there are various categories of scientist in the world. Those of the second and third category do their best but don't get very far. Those of the first category make important discoveries, basic to the progress of science. But then there are the geniuses like Galileo and Newton. Ettore Majorana was one of those.

Leonardo Scia Scia (a convinced atheist) described his reasons for writing The Mystery of Majorana.
'There is a conventional view of a scientist as someone necessarily indifferent or hostile to religion. But Ettore Majorana was a devout Catholic. His whole tragedy was a religious tragedy ... because he foresaw the problems to which Science was leading.'
As early as 1921 a German physicist, referring to Rutherford's atomic research had exclaimed: 'We are living on an island of Prolixin', adding that thank God the match hadn't yet been found to set it alight. (It obviously never occured to him that, once it had been found, one might still refrain from lighting it!) So why shouldn't Majorana, a physicist of genius who, fifteen years later, found himself confronted with the potential discovery of nuclear fission, have been able to realize that the match existed and so turned away from it in dismay and terror?
Majorana's sister Maria recalls that he often said at that time that physics was on the wrong track – or physicists – she

couldn't remember which. And he certainly was not referring to research as such but to the results achieved, or in the process of being achieved by this research. He was perhaps referring to life and death. Perhaps he meant to say what the German physicist Otto Hahn said at the beginning of 1939, when the 'discovery' of atomic energy was first discussed: 'But God cannot want that!'

AFFLICTION

It always strikes me, and it is very peculiar, that, whenever we see the image of indescribable and unutterable desolation of loneliness and poverty, and misery, the end and extreme of things, the thought of God comes into one's mind.

VINCENT VAN GOGH
Letter to his brother Theo

Those who have to stand by

I love Sophie more because she is ill. Illness, helplessness, is in itself a claim on love. We couldn't feel love for God Himself if He did not need our help. But those who are well and have to stand by and do nothing also need help, perhaps even more than the sick.

PENELOPE FITZGERALD
The Blue Flower

Ayez pitié de ceux qui s'aiment et qui ont été séparés, de ceux qui lutte contre les difficultés et qui ne cessent de tremper leur lèvres dans les amertumes de la vie.

Have pity on those who love one another and who have been separated, and on those who go on fighting against difficulties and who never stop suffering the bitterness of life.

HENRI ABBÉ PERREYVE

And on that day when every man's work shall be made manifest, it may be found, perhaps, that none have done Him better service than some of those who all through this life have been His ambassadors in bonds.

FRANCIS PAGET
The Spirit of Suffering

In a crisis

Let me give you three images, all of which have helped me on along 'many a flinty furlong'. At eighteen I learnt from Father Raymond Hecking, that grandly interior-minded Dominican, that I certainly could, with God's grace, give myself to Him, and strive to live my life long with Him and for Him. But that would mean winning and practising much desolation – that I would be climbing a mountain where, off and on, I might be enveloped in mist for days at a time, unable to see a foot in front of me. Had I noticed how mountaineers climb mountains? How they have a quiet, regular, short step - on the level it looks petty; but then this step they keep up, on and on, as they ascend, whilst the inexperienced townsman hurries along, and soon has to stop, dead beat with the climb. That such an expert mountaineer, when the thick mists come, halts and camps out under some slight cover brought with him, quietly smoking his pipe, and moving only when the mist has cleared away.

Then in my thirties I utilised another image, learnt in my Jesuit Retreats. How I was taking a long journey on board ship, with great storms pretty sure ahead of me; and how I must now select, and fix in my little cabin, some few but entirely appropriate things – a small trunk fixed up at one end, a chair that would keep its position, tumbler and glass that would do ditto: all this, simple, strong, and selected throughout in view of stormy weather. So would my spirituality have to be chosen and cultivated especially.

And lastly, in my forties, another image helped me – they are all three in pretty frequent use still. I am travelling on a camel across a huge desert. Windless days occur, and then all is well. But hurricanes of wind will come, unforeseen, tremendous. What to do then? It is very simple, but it takes much practice to do well at all. Dismount from the camel, fall prostrate face downwards on the sand, covering your head with your cloak. And lie thus, an hour, three hours, half a day: the sandstorm will go, and you will arise, and continue your journey as if nothing had happened. The old uncle has had many, many such sandstorms. How immensely useful they are!

You see, whether it be great cloud-mists on the mountain-side, or huge, mountain-high waves on the ocean, or blinding sandstorms in the desert: there is each time one crucial point – to form no conclusions, to take no decisions, to change nothing during such crises, and especially at such times, not to form any particular religious mood or idea in oneself. To turn gently to other things, to maintain a vague, general attitude of resignation – to be very meek, with oneself and with others: the crisis goes by, thus, with great fruit.

FRIEDRICH VON HUGEL
Letters to a Niece

Scorpion

'This night shall thy soul be required of thee'
My soul is never required of *me*.
It always has to be somebody else of course.
Will my soul be required of me tonight perhaps?

(I wonder what it will be like
To have one's soul required of one?
But all I can think of is the Out-Patients
  Department –
'Are you Mrs. Briggs, dear?'
'No, I am Scorpion')

I should like my soul to be required of me, so as
To waft over grass to the blue sea.
I am very fond of grass, I always have been, but there must
Be no cow, person or house to be seen.

Sea and *grass* must be quite empty
Other souls can find somewhere *else*.

O Lord God please come
And require the soul of thy Scorpion.

Scorpion so wishes to be gone.

STEVIE SMITH

O God that art the only refuge of unhappy man
Abiding in the faithfulness of heaven
Give me strong succour in this testing place.
O King protect Thy child from utter ruin,
Lest the weak faith surrender to the tyrant,
Facing innumerable blows alone.
Remember I am dust and wind and shadow,
And life as fleeting as the flower of grass.
But may the eternal mercy which hath shown from time of old,
Rescue thy servant from the jaws of the lion.
Thou who didst come from on high in the cloak of flesh,
Strike down the dragon with the two-edged sword.
Whereby our mortal flesh can war with the winds,
And strike down strongholds with our captain God.

THE VENERABLE BEDE

Is not man's life nothing but pressed service?
His time no better than hired drudgery?
Like the slave sighing for the shade,
Or the workman with no thought but his wages,
Months of delusion I have assigned to me,
Nothing for my own but nights of grief.
Lying in bed I wonder 'When will it be day?'
Risen I think 'How slowly evening comes!'
Restlessly I fret til twilight falls.
Swifter than a weaver's shuttle my days have passed.
And vanished leaving no hope behind,
Remember that my eyes wilt never again see joy.

THE BOOK OF JOB 7.1—7

Ah, my deare angrie Lord

Since thou doest love, yet strike,
Cast down, yet help afford;
Sure I will do the like.

I will complain, yet praise;
I will bewail, approve:
And all my soure-sweet days
I will lament and love.

GEORGE HERBERT

Germinal

In ancient shadows
Where childhood has strayed,
The world's great sorrows were born
And its heroes were made.
In the lost childhood of Judas
Christ was betrayed.

A. E.

Musée des Beaux Arts

About suffering they were never wrong,
The Old Masters: how well they understood
Its human position; how it takes place
    while someone else is eating, or opening
a window or just walking dully along.

W. H. AUDEN

The De Profundis

Out of the depths have I cried unto thee, O Lord!
Lord hear my voice!
Let thine ears be attentive to the voice of my supplication.
If thou, O Lord, should mark my iniquity,
Lord who would survive?
But with Thee is found forgiveness.
For this we revere Thee.

My soul is waiting for the Lord,
I count on his word.
My soul is longing for the Lord,
More than the watchman for daybreak.
Let the watchman count on daybreak,
And Israel on the Lord.
Because with the Lord there is mercy
And fullness of redemption,
Israel He will redeem from all its iniquity.

PSALM 130

Some pleasant inns

The Christian doctrine of suffering explains, I believe, a very
curious fact about the world we live in. The settled happiness
and security which we all desire, God witholds from us by the
very nature of the world, but joy, pleasure and merriment, He
has scattered broadcast. We are never safe, but we have plenty
of fun. The security we crave would teach us to rest our hearts
in this world, and pose an obstacle to our return to God ...
our Father refreshes us with some pleasant inns, but will not
encourage us to take them for home.

C. S. LEWIS
The Problem of Pain

THE MERIT OF SUFFERING

And our hope for you is firmly grounded; for we know that if you have part in the suffering, you have part also in the divine consolation.

ST PAUL TO THE CORINTHIANS

For with God it is impossible that anything how small so ever, if only it be suffered for God's sake, should pass without its reward.

THOMAS À KEMPIS
The Imitation of Christ

Unto Thee I commend myself and all that is mine, to be corrected; better it is to be punished here than hereafter. Thou knowest what is expedient for my profiting, and how greatly tribulation serves to slough off the rust of sins.

IBID.

The merit of suffering (whose value in the eyes of God who is so good and tender) far exceed, if accepted, all that we could lose by any weakness which arose from such suffering. As God has allowed you to suffer, you are more pleasing in His eyes, even though sinful, than if you were absolutely sinless, thanks to not having had to bear suffering. Praise God! All this is really true and without the slightest doubt.

ABBÉ DE TOURVILLE
Letters of Direction

You must find strength in the thought that suffering accepted in the right spirit has the most valuable, the most lasting and the happiest results. Suffering assures us that we are associated with the work of Our Lord and united to Him. We must believe it and console ourselves with the reflection that, in spite of appearances, the most difficult moments are when we are most fruitfully alive. Besides, they will pass. It is hard: but God knows how hard.

TEILHARD DE CHARDIN

Robert Speaight, Teilhard de Chardin: A Biography

God has promised us not that we shall be free from crosses, rather do they form a ladder by which the soul mounts upwards: but that He will abide with His faithful servant through them all, and be his rock, his strong foundation.

ANON.

Our loves and our desires

It is our loves and our desires that determine our pains. If our supreme love is the pleasure of the body, then our greatest pain is loss of health; if our supreme love is wealth, then our greatest fear is poverty; if our supreme love is God, then our greatest fear is sin.

ARCHBISHOP FULTON SHEEN

The Way to Happiness

Some day, in the next world, if not in this, we shall pour out our hearts in thanksgiving to Him, because He did not let us have an easy life, because He went on trusting us to persevere in His own way, the narrow way, the way of the Cross, the way of habitual prayer, in spite of all its difficulties; because He called on us to attain to a life of communion with Himself, through the greatest efforts we were capable of making.

ANON.

GRIEF

'To Thee have I cried from the ends of the earth.'

PSALM 61

Who is this that cries from the ends of the earth? Who is this
one man who reaches to the extremities of the universe? Christ's
whole body groans in pain. Until the end of the world, when
pain will pass away, this man groans and cries to God. Thou
didst cry in thy day and thy days have passed away; another took
thy place and cried out in his day. Thou here, he there and
another there ... There is one man who reaches to the end
of time, and those who cry out are always his members.

ST AUGUSTINE

Sermons

Catherine of Aragon to her husband Henry VIII, from the Tower of London:
My Lord and dear Husband,
I commend myself to you.

The hour of my death draweth fast on and the tender love
I have for you forceth me, with a few words, to put you in
remembrance of the health and safeguard of your soul which
you ought to prefer before all worldly matters, and before the
care and tendering of your body for the which you have cast
me into many miseries and yourself into many cares. For my

part I pardon you all, yea I do wish and devoutly pray God that He will also pardon you.

Lastly do I vow, that mine eyes desire you above all things.

Letter of a miner's wife whose husband was killed in the Whitehaven mining disaster in 1914
God took my man but I could never forget him he was the best man that ever lived at least I thought that maybe it was just that I got the right kind of man. We had been married for 25 years and they were hard years at that, many a thing we both done without for the sake of the children. We had 11 and if I had him back I would live the same life over again, just when we were beginning to stand on our feet I lost him. I can't get over it when I think of him how happy he was that morning going to work and telling me he would hurry home, but I have been waiting a long time now. At night when I am sitting and I hear clogs coming down the street I just sit and wait hoping they are coming to my door, then they go right on and my heart is broke.

IRIS ORIGO
The Vagabond Path

Giovanni Falcone, his wife and three of his police escort were blown up on their way to Palermo airport. Falcone had up to that date, put 342 Mafiosi into prison, of whom 19 were given life. The funeral of [the judge] Falcone, his wife, Francesca Morvillo, and three of his escorts, was held on a rainy day in May 1992 in the church of San Domenico [Palermo] ... People have never forgotten the moment the young widow of a Sicilian policeman, a delicate and implacable young woman in black,

ordered the country's leaders to their knees. She spoke
about her dead husband, more to herself than the mourners
crowding the church. 'He was so beautiful' she said. 'He had
such beautiful legs.' She spoke some further words she'd
prepared with a priest's help. In the emotion of the moment
she came out loud and clear but in fragments:

My Vito Schifano,
Why are the mafiosi still inside the state ...
I pardon you
but get down on your knees ...
but they don't want to change ...
they don't change ... too much blood ...
there's no love here
there's no love here there's no love here at all.

PETER ROBB
Midnight in Sicily

Evil dwells in the heart of the criminal without being felt there.
It is felt in the heart of the man who is afflicted and innocent.

SIMONE WEIL
Waiting on God

Slave camps under the flag of freedom, massacres justified by
philanthropy, or the taste for the superhuman, cripple judgement.
On the day when crime puts on the apparel of innocence,
through a reversal peculiar to our age, it is innocence which is
called upon to justify itself.

ALBERT CAMUS
The Rebel

A weed called tyranny

Whenever a people, thirsting for liberty, discovers that its leaders will give it whatever it seeks, even to the point of intoxication, then if Government resists its more extreme demands it is called tyranny, and those who show discipline to their superiors are called lackeys.

The father, filled with fear, comes to treat his son as an equal, and is not respected. The master no longer reprimands his servants and is mocked by them. The young claim the same consideration as the old, who, in no way wishing to seem severe, yield to them.

In the name of liberty, no one is any longer respected. In the midst of this licence there flourishes a weed called tyranny.

PLATO
The Republic

Elizabeth I to the Judges of the Realm

Have a care over my people. You have my people – do that which I ought to do. They are my people. Every man oppresseth them and spoileth them without mercy. They cannot defend themselves. See unto them, see unto them, for they are my charge. I charge you, even as God has charged me.

Daily prayer said by the Speaker's Chaplain in the House of Commons

Never lead the nation wrongly through love of power, desire to please or unworthy ideals but, laying aside all private interests and prejudices, keep in mind the responsibility to seek to improve the condition of all mankind.

I and the public know
What all school children learn,
Those to whom evil is done
Do evil in return.

W. H. AUDEN
A Certain World

DEATH

*No morir, no morir, Seneca, no. Io per me non vo. Questa vita e
dolce troppo.*
Don't die, don't die, Seneca. For my part, I do not want to
die. This life is too sweet.

GIUSEPPE MONTEVERDI
Incoronazione di Popea

Even memory is not necessary for love
'Even now,' the Abbess thought, 'Almost nobody remembers
Esteban and Pepita but myself. Camilla alone remembers her
uncle Pio and her son; this woman, her mother. But soon we
shall die and all the memories of those five will have been
enough; all those impulses of love return to the love that made
them. Even memory is not necessary for love. There is a land
of the living and a land of the dead, and the bridge is love, the
only survival, the only meaning.'

THORNTON WILDER
The Bridge of San Luis Rey

Since I am coming to that Holy roome
Where with Thy Quire of Saints, for ever more
I shall be made Thy music:
                As I come
I tune the Instrument here at the door,
And what I must do then, think here before.

JOHN DONNE
Hymn to God, my God, in my Sicknesse

Et, à l'heure de ma mort, soyez le refuge de mon ame étonné, et
recevez-là dans le sein de Votre miséricorde.
And at the hour of my death, receive my astonished soul in
Your merciful arms.

ST MARGARET MARY

J'ai voulu devant vous,
Exposant mes remords,
Par un chemin plus lent
Descendre chez les morts.
Exposing to you, my remorse,
I would have wished,
By a slave road
To go down among the dead.

JEAN RACINE
Phèdre

Death has a look of finality;
We think we lose something but if it were not for
Death we should have nothing to lose.
Existence
Because unlimited, would merely be existence
Without incarnate value.

LOUIS MACNEICE

St Thérèse of Lisieux when she was dying:
I am suffering, but only for an instant. It is because we think of
the past and the future that we become discouraged and fall
into despair.

ST THÉRÈSE OF LISIEUX
The Story of a Soul, trans. Ronald Knox

111

How hard it is to die

The first time he went missing there was panic. They searched the bathroom, all the other rooms, and when they reached the stone hallway they found the front door was open.

They found him leaning in exhaustion on a wooden post at the back of the house, staring into the emptiness of the meadow … It was no longer empty but filling with a fresh growth, a faint blue tinge in the rich green of the young grass. To die was never to look on all this again. It would live in others' eyes but not in his. He had never realized when he was in the midst of confident life what an amazing glory he was part of. He heard his name being called frantically. Then he was scolded and led back to the house. He stopped stubbornly before the door. 'I never knew how hard it was to die,' he said simply.

JOHN MCGAHERN
Amongst Women

I know you want to keep on living. You do not want to die. You want to pass from this life to another in such a way that you will not rise again as a dead man but fully alive and transformed. This is what you desire. This is the deepest human feeling. The soul itself mysteriously wishes and instinctively desires it.

ST AUGUSTINE
Sermons

No man can die for another

The challenge of death comes to us all and no one can die for another. Everyone must fight his own battle with death by himself, alone ... I will not be with you then, nor you with me.

MARTIN LUTHER
Eight Sermons at Wittenberg

A poor untidy thing

This day we're facing death maybe. And death should be a poor untidy thing, though it is a queen that dies.

J. M. SYNGE
Deidre of the Sorrows

The Tomb, in Westminster Abbey of Elizabeth I and Mary Tudor

Consorts in the Kingdom and in the tomb
Here we rest, Elizabeth and Mary,
Sisters in the hope of Resurrection

Loved wife of C. S. Lewis

Here the whole world (stars, water, air,
And field and forest, as they were
Perfected in a single mind)
Like cast-off clothes, was left behind
In ashes, yet with hope that she
Re-born from holy poverty,
In lenten lands, hereafter may
Resume them on her Easter day.

Epitaph for his brother John Paul

Sweet brother if I do not sleep,
My eyes are flowers for your tomb.
And if I cannot eat my bread
My fast shall live like willows where you died.
If in the heat I find no water for my thirst,
My thirst shall turn to springs for you, poor brother,
Come, in my labour find a resting place,
And in my sorrows lay your head,
Or rather, take my life and blood,
And buy yourself a better bed.
Or take my breath and take my death,
And buy yourself a better rest.

THOMAS MERTON
Monica Furlong, Merton: A Biography

Seigneur de mon enfance et Seigneur de mon fin
Lord of my childhood and Lord of my end

TEILHARD DE CHARDIN

Martyrs

The heroism of the martyrs consisted of just this: they really
loved this life; yet they weighed it up. They thought of how
much they should love the things eternal if they were capable
of so much love for the things which pass away.

ST AUGUSTINE
Peter Brown, St Augustine of Hippo

The falcon hath borne my mate away

*Here is a haunting lament for the dead Christ, written in the late
fifteenth century. There is something strange and even terrible in the
lilting refrain. But in this simple piece of poetry you seem to hear, for
a few minutes, those far-off medieval voices through the darkness of
time.*

Lully, lulley, lully, lulley,
The fawcon hath borne my mak away.

He bare him up, he bare him down,
He bare him in to an orchard brown.
Lully, lulley, lully, lulley,
The fawcon hath borne my mak away,

In that orchard ther was an hall,
That was hanged with purpill and pall.
Lully, lulley, lully, lulley,
The fawcon hath borne my mak away.

And in that hall ther was a bed,
It was hanged with gold so red.
Lully, lulley, lully, lulley,
The fawcon hath borne my mak away.

And in that bed ther lythe a knight,
His woundes bleeding day and night.
Lully, lulley, lully, lulley,
The fawcon hath borne my mak away.

By that bedes side kneleth a may,
And she wepeth both night and day.
Lully, lulley, lully, lulley,
The fawcon hath borne my mak away.

And by that bedes side ther stondeth a stone,
Corpus Christ! written thereon.
Lully, lulley, lully, lulley,
The fawcon hath borne my mak away.

A MAIDEN
late 15th century

THE PASSION OF CHRIST

Woefully array'd
My blood, man
For thee ran,
It cannot be array'd,
Woefully array'd.

JOHN SKELTON

The face of God Himself

Now I beg you consider that that face, so ruthlessly smitten, was
the face of God Himself; the brows bloody with thorns, the
sacred body exposed to view and lacerated with the scourge,
the hands nailed to the cross, and afterwards, the sides pierced
with the spear; it was the blood, and the sacred flesh, and the
hands, and the temples, and the side, and the feet of God
Himself, which the frenized multitude then gazed upon.

CARDINAL NEWMAN
Plain and Parochial Sermons

Who has believed our message?
And to whom has the arm of the Lord been revealed?
He grew up, before Him like a tender shoot,
And like a root out of dry ground.
He had no beauty or majesty to attract us to him,
Nothing in his appearance that we should desire him.
He was despised and rejected by men.
A man of sorrows and familiar with grief.

Like one from whom men hid their faces
He was despised and we esteemed him not.
Surely he took up our infirmities and carried our sorrows,
Yet we considered him stricken by God
Smitten by Him and afflicted.

But he was pierced for our transgressions,
He was crushed for our iniquities,
The punishment that brought us peace was upon him,
We all, like sheep, have gone astray,
Each of us has turned to his own way,

And the Lord laid on him the iniquity of us all.
He was oppressed and afflicted yet he did not open his mouth.
He was led like a Lamb to the slaughter,
And as the sheep before her shearer is silent
So he did not open his mouth.
By oppression and judgement he was taken away,
And who can speak of his descendants?
For he was cut off from the land of the living.

ISAIAH 53.1—6

The seven last words

These were not just the words of a dying man; they were
more. The human voice of the dying Christ was speaking, of
divine thoughts and attitudes. Each of these last words has the
power to transform lives, for they are the Word of God. They
reveal their secrets, slowly, if we meditate on them and pray.

CARDINAL HUME
To Be a Pilgrim

We read in the Gospels:
Luke 23.33

> And when they reached the place which is named after a
> skull, they crucified him there – Jesus meanwhile was saying,
> 'Father forgive them; they know not what they do.' And
> they divided his garments among themselves by lot.

Luke 23.39–43

> And one of the two thieves who hung there fell to blaspheming
> against him … But the other said to Jesus, 'Lord, remember
> me when thou comest into thy kingdom.' And Jesus said him,
> 'I promise thee, this day thou shall be with me in Paradise.'

John 19.35

> Meanwhile his mother had taken her stand beside the Cross
> of Jesus. And Jesus seeing his mother there, and the disciple
> too whom he loved, standing by, said 'Woman, this is thy
> son.' Then he said to his disciple, 'This is thy mother.' And
> from that hour the disciple took her into his own keeping.

Matthew 27.45

From the sixth hour onwards there was darkness over all the earth until the ninth hour; and about the ninth hour Jesus cried out in a loud voice, 'My God, my God why hast thou forsaken me?'

John 19.28–30

And now Jesus knew well that all was achieved which the Scripture had demanded for its accomplishment and he said, 'I thirst.' There was a jar there full of vinegar, so they filled a sponge with the vinegar and put it on a stick of hyssop, and brought it close to his mouth. Jesus drank the vinegar and said, 'It is achieved.'

Luke 23. 46

And Jesus said, crying out with a loud voice, 'Father, into thy hands I commend my spirit', and yielded up his spirit as he said it.

If I love know

When I see on the cross
Jesus my love,
And beside him standing,
Mary and John,
And His back scourged,
And His side gashed,
For the love of men,
Well ought I to weep,
And sins for to leave,
If I love know,
If I love know.

FOURTEENTH CENTURY

The Stations of the Cross

1. The first station – Jesus Christ is condemned to death
2. The second station – Jesus receives the cross
3. Jesus falls the first time under the weight of the cross
4. Jesus is met by His mother
5. The cross is laid on Simon of Cyrene
6. The face of Jesus is wiped by Veronica
7. Jesus falls a second time
8. The women of Jerusalem mourn for Our Lord
9. Jesus falls the third time under the cross
10. Jesus is stripped of his garments
11. Jesus is nailed to the cross
12. Jesus dies upon the cross
13. Jesus is laid in the arms of his mother
14. Jesus is laid in the tomb

THE RESURRECTION

*In the 1970s the then Bishop of Durham told his flock and the world
in general that the Resurrection was a story, a charming fable,
something which the faithful were not required to believe in. At this
the late Lord Hailsham spoke up. He said he was indignant that a
leading churchman should come out with such a statement.
He himself preferred to believe in the gospels of Matthew, Mark, Luke
and John because they were there at the Resurrection and the Bishop
of Durham was not.*

Here is a small part of St Paul's great meditation on the Resurrection:

**For what I received I passed onto you as of first
importance, that Christ died for our sins according
to the scriptures, that He was buried, that He was
raised again on the third day according to the scriptures and that he appeared to Peter, and then to the
twelve. After that He appeared to more than five
hundred of the brothers at the same time, most of
whom are still living …**

**But if it is preached that Christ has been raised
from the dead, how can some of you say that there is
no resurrection of the dead? If there is no resurrection of the dead, then not even Christ has been
raised, our preaching is useless and so is your faith.**

ST PAUL TO THE CORINTHIANS 15.3—7,12—15

The pilgrim

Give me my scallop shell of quiet,
My staff of Faith to walk upon;
My scrip of joy, immortal diet
My bottle of salvation;
My gown of glory, hope's true gage;
And thus I'll make my pilgrimage.
Blood must be my body's balmer –
No other balm will there be given –
Christ, my soul, like a white palmer,
Travels to the land of heaven;
Over the silver mountains,
Where spring the nectar fountains,
And there I'll kiss
The bowl of bliss,
And drink my eternal fill
On every milken hill:
My soul will be adry before,
But after it will ne'er thirst more.

WALTER RALEIGH

We first invoke God Himself, not in loud words, but in the way of prayer which is always in our power, leaning in soul towards Him by aspiration, alone with the Alone.

PLOTINUS
Dean Inge, The Philosophy of Plotinus

Prayer is easy

Ordinary Catholics are praying when they do not think they are. They are praying when they offer implicitly all they are doing to God.

VINCENT MCNABB
The Craft of Prayer

My one prayer

And for those dear to me my one prayer is that they may see God.

CARDINAL NEWMAN

THE OUR FATHER

The great prayer
We are speaking of 'the Our Father', as the great prayer Our
Lord has revealed to the world.

We have forms of Faith – the Apostles Creed, the Nicene
Creed; a form of Morals – the Ten Commandments; and now
we have the form of Prayer. That being Divine, has never been
touched … the Church would never add to the form of the
Prayer.

As it is formed by eternal wisdom, we need not be at all
surprised that it offers a great deal to the intelligence. The
intelligence is very important. If the intelligence is wrong, the
will can be very wilful. So that if this prayer appeals first of all
to our intelligence, that is the Divine doing.

VINCENT MCNABB
The Craft of Prayer

This model prayer contains a statement of our rights. We go to
God and demand something from Him, like hunger-marchers
demanding bread. God has told us to do it. We begin to impose
our will on God. He loves to do our will if it is a good will. One
of the old proverbs says that 'Humility imposes its will on God.'
Granted that we love God, He is constantly doing our will.

IBID.

125

... and so being our Father, He must bear with us, however great our offences. If we return to Him He must pardon us as He pardoned the prodigal son. He must comfort us in our trials, and must sustain us as He is better than any earthly father. He must cherish us and support us: and at the last He must make us heirs to the kingdom along with His Son.

ST TERESA OF AVILA
The Way of Perfection

The words of the Lord's Prayer are perfectly pure. Anyone who repeats the Lord's Prayer with no other intention than to bring to bear upon the words themselves the fullest attention of which he is capable, is absolutely certain of being delivered in this way from a part, however small, of the evil he harbours within him. It is the same if one contemplates the Blessed Sacrament with no other thought except that Christ is there, and so on.

SIMONE WEIL
Waiting on God

Notre père qui est aux cieux, restez-y,
Et nous resterons sur la terre qui est si jolie.
Our Father, who art in heaven, please stay there,
And let us stay on the earth which is so pretty

JACQUES PRÉVERT

The Eight Beatitudes

1. Blessed are the poor in spirit: for theirs is the kingdom of heaven.
2. Blessed are the meek: for they shall inherit the earth.
3. Blessed are they that mourn: for they shall be comforted.
4. Blessed are they that hunger and thirst after justice: for they shall be filled.
5. Blessed are the merciful: for they shall obtain mercy.
6. Blessed are the pure of heart: for they shall see God.
7. Blessed are the peacemakers: for they shall be called the children of God.
8. Blessed are they that suffer persecution for justice's sake: for theirs is the kingdom of heaven.

MATTHEW 5.3—11

God's grandeur

The world is charged with the grandeur of God.
It will flame out, like shining from shook foil;
It gathers to a greatness, like the ooze of oil
Crushed. Why do men then now not reck his rod?
Generations have trod, have trod, have trod;
And all is seared with trade; blear'd, smeared with toil;
And wears man's smudge and shares man's smell: the soil
Is bare now, nor can foot feel, being shod.

And for all this, nature is never spent;
There lives the dearest freshness deep down things;
And though the last lights off the black West went
Oh, morning, at the brown brink eastward springs –

Because the Holy Ghost over the bent
World broods with warm breast and with ah!
bright wings.

GERARD MANLEY HOPKINS

SILENCE AND SOLITUDE

Spirit of Silences, remake me.

SIEGFRIED SASSOON

I am living in the wilderness of Calabria, far removed from any habitation. I can't begin to tell you how charming and pleasant it is. The temperatures are mild and the air is healthy; a broad plain stretches between the mountains along their entire length bursting with scented meadows and flowery fields. One can hardly describe the impression made by the gently rolling hills on all sides, their cool and shady valleys tucked away, and such an abundance of refreshing springs – brooks and streams ... What benefits and what divine exultation the silence and solitude of the desert hold in store for those who love it.

ST BRUNO
Letter to Raoul le Verd

A vast, bright solitude

And when he went to sea and faced a vast, bright solitude, blue sky and cold water, he thanked God with such a shock of gratitude and grief that he never got over it. He took to worshipping God inwardly all the time, seeing God's work everywhere, now that His servant was seaborne, and upright and paid no man rent.

MELISSA FAYE GREENE
Praying for Sheetrock

Only one thing is necessary: solitude. To withdraw into oneself and not to meet anyone for hours – that is what we must arrive at. To be alone as a child is alone when grown-ups come and go.

RAINER MARIA RILKE
Letters to a Young Poet

Contemplation in a world of action

I am not defending a phony 'hermit-mystique', but some of us have to be alone to be ourselves. Call it privacy if you like. But we have thinking to do and work to do which demands a certain silence and aloneness. We need time to do our job of meditation and creation.

THOMAS MERTON

The present condition of the world is diseased. If I were a doctor and were asked for my advice I would answer 'Create silence, bring men to silence: the word of God cannot be heard in the world today. And if it is blazoned forth with noise, so that it can be heard even in the midst of other noise, then it is no longer the word of God. Therefore create silence.'

SØREN KIERKEGAARD

Miracles

'Where there is great love there are always miracles,' the bishop said, 'One might almost say that an apparition is human vision corrected by divine love. I do not see you as you really are, Joseph; I see you through my affection for you. The miracles of the Church seem to me to rest not so much upon faces or voices or healing power coming suddenly near us from far off, but upon our perceptions being made finer, so that for a moment our eyes can see and our ears can hear what is there about us always.'

WILLA CATHER
Death Comes for the Archbishop

The Ten Commandments

1. Thou shalt not have strange gods before Me. Thou shalt not make to thyself any graven thing; nor the likeness of anything that is in heaven above, or in the earth beneath, nor of those things that are in the waters under the earth. Thou shalt not adore them nor serve them.
2. Thou shalt not take the name of the Lord thy God in vain.
3. Remember that thou keep holy the Sabbath day.
4. Honour thy father and thy mother.
5. Thou shalt not kill.
6. Thou shalt not commit adultery.
7. Thou shalt not steal.
8. Thou shalt not bear false witness against thy neighbour.
9. Thou shalt not covet thy neighbour's wife.
10. Thou shalt not covet thy neighbour's goods.

CATECHISM OF THE CATHOLIC CHURCH

The Greatest Commandment

Thou shalt love the Lord thy God with thy whole heart, and
with thy whole soul, and with thy whole mind, and with thy
whole strength ... And thou shalt love thy neighbour as thyself.

1. Mind refers to knowledge
2. Heart refers to attention
3. Soul refers to affections and desires
4. Strength refers to external performance

... and all these powers must be employed in loving God.

ST THOMAS AQUINAS
Summa Theologica

Boredom

A certain power of enduring boredom is essential to a happy
life. The lives of most great men have not been exciting except
at a few moments. A generation which is unable to endure
boredom will be a generation of little men.

BERTRAND RUSSELL
The Conquest of Happiness

Longing for certainties

The intelligent and shrewd easily detect in religious people the
immature, if wholly understandable longing for certainties,
whether in what to believe or in what to do or not do.

SISTER RUTH BURROWS
Before the Living God

132

Oh what a dusty answer gets the soul when hot for certainties
in this our life.

GEORGE MEREDITH

The soul and the dental apparatus

My soul would have been quite different if I had not stammered
or if I had been four or five inches taller. I am slightly
prognathus: in my childhood they did not know that this
could be remedied by a gold band worn while the jaw is still
malleable; if they had, my countenance would have been of a
different caste, the reaction towards me of my fellow men would
have been different, and therefore my disposition, my attitude
towards them would have been different too. But what sort of
thing is this soul that can be modified by a dental apparatus?

SOMERSET MAUGHAM

I cannot understand what is meant by 'mind' and how this
differs from 'soul' or spirit'. They all seem the same to me ...

ST TERESA OF AVILA
A. Allison Peers, The Life of St Teresa of Avila

The Right to Life

*The Second Vatican Council solemnly reaffirmed the dignity of the
human person, and in a special way his or her right to life. The
Council therefore condemned crimes against life 'such as any type
of murder, genocide, abortion, euthanasia or wilful suicide'.*

In modern society, in which even the fundamental values of human life are often called into question, cultural change exercises an influence upon the way of looking at suffering and death; moreover, medicine has increased its capacity to cure and prolong life in particular circumstances, which sometimes gives rise to moral problems. Thus people living in this situation experience no little anxiety about the meaning of advanced old age and death. They also begin to wonder whether they have the right to obtain for themselves or their fellow men an 'easy death', which would shorten suffering and which seems to them more in harmony with human dignity.

The considerations set forth in the present Document concern in the first place all those who place their faith and hope in Christ, who, through his life, death and resurrection, has given a new meaning to existence and especially the death of the Christian.

As for those who profess other religions, many will agree with us that faith in God the Creator and Lord of life – if they share this belief – confers a lofty dignity upon every human person and guarantees respect for him or her.

It is hoped that this Declaration will meet with the approval of many people of good will who, philosophical or ideological differences notwithstanding, have nevertheless a lively awareness of the rights of the human person. These rights have often in fact been proclaimed in recent years through declarations issued by International Congresses.

The value of life
Most people regard life as something sacred and hold that nobody may dispose of it at will, but believers see in life

something greater, namely a gift of God's love, which they are called upon to preserve and make fruitful. And it is this latter consideration which gives rise to the following consequences:

1. No one can make an attempt on the life of an innocent person without opposing God's love for that person, without violating a fundamental right, and therefore without committing a crime of the utmost gravity. *(The problems of the death penalty and of war, which involve specific considerations, do not concern the present subject.)*
2. Everyone has the duty to lead his or her life in accordance with God's plan. That life is trusted to the individual as a good that must bear fruit already in this life, but that finds its perfection only in eternal life.
3. Intentionally causing one's own death, or suicide, is therefore equally as wrong as murder; such an action on the part of person is to be considered a rejection of God's sovereign and loving plan. Furthermore, suicide is also often a refusal of love for self, the denial of the natural instinct to live, a flight from the duties of justice and charity to one's neighbour, to various communities or to the whole of society *although, as is generally recognized, there are psychological factors present that can diminish responsibility or even completely remove it.*

However, one must clearly distinguish suicide from that sacrifice of one's life whereby for a higher cause, such as God's glory, the salvation of souls, or the service of one's brothers, a person offers his or her own life or puts it in danger (cf. John 15.14).

Euthanasia

In order that the question of euthanasia can be properly dealt with, it is first necessary to define the words used.

In ancient times *euthanasia* meant *an easy death*. Ultimately, the word euthanasia is used in a more particular sense to mean 'mercy killing' for the purpose of putting an end to extreme suffering, or saving abnormal babies, the mentally ill, or the incurably sick, from the prolongation, perhaps for many years, of a miserable life, which could impose too heavy a burden on their families or on society.

It is therefore necessary to state clearly in what sense the word is used in the present document.

By euthanasia is understood an action or omission which of itself or by intention causes death, in order that all suffering may in this way be eliminated. Euthanasia's terms of reference. therefore, are to be found in the intention of the will and in the methods used.

It is necessary to state firmly that nothing and no one can in any way permit the killing of an innocent human being, whether a foetus or embryo, an infant or adult, an old person or one suffering from an incurable disease, or one who is dying.

Furthermore no one is permitted to ask for this act of killing, either for himself or for another person entrusted to his or her care, nor can he or she consent to it, either explicitly or implicitly.

Nor can any authority legitimately recommend or permit such an action. For it is a question of the violation of the divine law, an offence against the dignity of the human person, a crime against life, and an attack on humanity.

It may happen that by reason of prolonged and barely tolerable pain, for deeply personal or other reasons, people may be led to believe that they can legitimately ask for death or obtain it from others. Although in these cases the guilt of the individual may be reduced or completely absent, nevertheless the error of judgement into which the conscience falls, perhaps in good faith, does not change the nature of this act of killing, which will always in itself be something to be rejected.

The pleas of gravely ill people who sometimes ask for death are not to be understood as implying a true desire for euthanasia, in fact it is almost always a case of an anguished plea for help and love. What a sick person needs, besides medical care, is love, and the human and supernatural warmth with which the sick person can and ought to be surrounded by all those close to him or her, parents and children, doctors and nurses.

The meaning of suffering for Christians and the use of painkillers
Death does not always come in dramatic circumstances after barely tolerable sufferings. Nor do we have to think only in terms of extreme cases. Numerous testimonies which confirm one another lead to the conclusion that nature itself has made provision to render more bearable at the moment of death separations which would be terribly painflul to a person in full health. Hence it is that a prolonged illness, advanced old age, or a certain state of loneliness or neglect, can bring about psychological conditions which facilitate the acceptance of death.

Nevertheless the fact remains that death, often preceded or accompanied by severe and prolonged suffering, is something which naturally causes people anguish.

Physical suffering is certainly an unavoidable element of the
human condition; on the biological level, it constitutes a warning
of which no one denies the usefulness; but since it affects the
human psychological make-up, it often exceeds its own biological
use, and can become so severe as to cause the desire to remove
it at any cost.

According to Christian teaching, however, suffering, especially
suffering during the last moments of life, has a special place in
God's saving plan; it is in fact a sharing in Christ's Passion and
a union with the redeeming sacrifice which He offered in
obedience to the Father's will. Therefore ... some Christians
prefer to moderate their use of painkillers in order to accept,
voluntarily at least, some of the sufferings of Christ crucified
(cf. Matthew 27.34). Nevertheless it would be imprudent
to impose a heroic way of acting as a general rule. On the
contrary, human and Christian prudence suggest for the
majority of sick people the use of medicines capable of
alleviating or suppressing pain, even though these may cause,
as a secondary effect, semiconsciousness and reduce lucidity.

*Declaration of Pope Pius XII in answer to a group of doctors who had
put the question:* 'Is the suppression of pain and consciousness
by the use of narcotics permitted by religion and morality to
the doctor and the patient (even at the approach of death, and
if one foresees that the use of narcotics will shorten life)?'
The Pope said: 'If no other means exist, and if, in the given
circumstances, this does not prevent the carrying out of other
religious and moral duties: Yes.'

However, painkillers which cause unconsciousness need
special consideration. For a person not only has to be able to

satisfy his or her moral duties and family obligations; they have to prepare themselves with full consciousness for meeting Christ. Thus Pius XII warns: 'It is not right to deprive the dying person of consciousness without a serious reason.'

Due proportion in the use of remedies
Today it is very important, at the moment of death, to protect both the human person and the Christian concept of life against a technological attitude which threatens to become an abuse. Thus some people speak of the 'right to die', which is an expression that does not mean the right to procure death by one's own hand or by means of someone else, as one pleases, but rather the right to die peacefully with human and Christian dignity.

Everyone has the duty to care for his or her own health or seek such care from others. Those whose task it is to take care of the sick must do so conscientiously and administer the remedies that seem necessary or useful.

However, is it necessary in all circumstances to have recourse to all possible remedies?

1. If there are no other sufficient remedies it is permitted, with the patient's consent, to have recourse to the means provided by the most advanced medical techniques, even if these are still at the experimental stage and are not without a certain risk. By accepting them, the patient can even show generosity in the service of mankind.
2. It is also permitted, with the patients consent, to interrupt those means, where the results fall short of expectations. But for such a decision taken of the reasonable wishes of the patient and the patient's family, as also of the advice of

doctors who are specially competent in the matter.

The latter may in particular judge that the investment in instruments and personnel is disproportionate to the results foreseen; they may also judge that the techniques applied impose on the patient strain or suffering out of proportion with the benefits which he or she may gain from such techniques.

3. It is also permissible to make do with the normal means that medicine can offer. Therefore no one can impose on anyone the obligation to have recourse to a technique which is already in use but which carries a risk or is burdensome. Such a refusal is not the equivalent of suicide; on the contrary, it should be considered as an acceptance of the human condition, or a wish to avoid the application of a medical procedure disproportionate to the results that can be expected, or a desire not to impose excessive expense on the family or the community.

4. When inevitable death is imminent in spite of the means used, it is permitted in conscience to take the decision to refuse all forms of treatment that would only secure a precarious and burdensome prolongation of life, so long as the normal care due to the sick person in similar cases is not interrupted. In such circumstances the doctor has no reason to reproach himself for failing to help the person in danger.

Pope John Paul II approved this Declaration adopted at the meeting of the Sacred Congregation for the Doctrine of the Faith, and ordered its publication.

VATICAN II: GAUDIUM ET SPES
Rome, 5 May, 1980

THE CHILD

Heir to the world

All appeared new and strange at first, inexpressibly rare and delightful and beautiful. I was a little stranger, which, at my entrance into the world, was saluted and surrounded by innumerable joys. My knowledge was Divine. I knew, by intuition, those things which since my apostasy I collected again by the highest reason. My very ignorance was advantageous. All things were spotless and pure and glorious; yea, and infinitely mine and joyful and precious. I knew not that there were any sins or complaints or laws. I dreamed not of poverties, contentions or vices.

All Heaven and Earth did sing my Creator's praises, and could not make more melody to Adam than to me. All time was Eternity and a perpetual Sabbath ... The corn was orient and immortal wheat, which never should be reaped nor was ever sown. I had thought it stood from everlasting ... the gates were at first the end of the world. The green trees, when I first saw them through the gates, transported and ravished me, and their sweetness and unusual beauty made my heart to leap, and almost mad with ecstasy, they were such strange and wonderful things ... Boys and girls tumbling and playing in the streets were moving jewels. I knew not that they were born and should die; but all things abided eternally as they were in their proper places ... The city seemed to stand in Eden or to be built in Heaven. The streets were mine, the

skies were mine, and all the world was mine and I the only
spectator and enjoyer of it.

THOMAS TRAHERNE

Century III

You are a marvel

Sometimes I look around me with complete dismay. In the
confusion that afflicts the world today, I see a disrespect for
the very values of life. Beauty is all about us, but how many
are blind to it. They look at the wonder of this earth and seem
to see nothing. People move about hectically but give little
thought to where they are going. They seek excitement for its
mere sake, as if they were lost and desperate. They take little
pleasure in the natural and quiet and simple things of life. Each
second we live in a new and unique moment of the universe, a
moment that never was before and will never be again.

And what do we teach our children in school? We teach
them that two and two make four and that Paris is in France.
We should say to each one of them 'Do you know what you
are? You are a marvel. You are unique. In all the world there is
no other child exactly like you. And look at your body – what
a wonder it is! Your legs, your arms, your cunning fingers, the
way you move. You may become a Shakespeare, a Michelangelo,
a Beethoven. You have the capacity for anything.'

PABLO CASALS

Joys and Sorrows: Reflections

Children sweeten Labours; but they make misfortune more bitter; they increase the Cares of Life; but they mitigate the Remembrance of Death.

FRANCIS BACON
Essays

The strongest and most terrible thing on earth – though they never know it – is the love of children ... I will have all my little children pray for yours, and that to our Blessed Lady who never fails us unhappy children of hers.

HILAIRE BELLOC
Christopher Sykes, Nancy: The Life of Lady Astor

Fear not, the child of so many tears cannot perish.

ST AMBROSE TO ST MONICA

Your love for your children
Your love for your children has eaten up all your reserves of generosity and sacrifice. They stop you from seeing other people. It isn't only me you have turned away from but the rest of the world. To God Himself you can't talk about anything else except their health, their future.

FRANÇOIS MAURIAC
Le Noeud de Vipères

Lay baptism

Any person whether man, woman or child, may baptise an
infant in danger of death, and ought to do so, without waiting
to send for a priest.

Take common water, pour it on the head or face of the child
and while pouring it say:

I baptise thee in the name of the Father, and of the Son and of
the Holy Spirit.

THE DAILY MISSAL

Abortion

Human life must be respected and protected from the moment
of conception. From the first moment of his existence a human
being must be recognized as having the rights of a person –
among which is the inviolable right of every innocent being to
life.

Formal cooperation in an abortion constitutes a grave offence.
The Church attaches the canonical penalty to this crime
against human life. It does not thereby intend to restrict the
scope of mercy. Rather she makes clear the gravity of the
crime   committed, the irreparable harm done to the innocent
who is put to death, as well as to the parents and the whole of
society.

CATECHISM OF THE CATHOLIC CHURCH

Mankind owes the child

Peter Mahon, expelled from the Labour party after standing as Britain's first anti-abortion candidate, spoke as follows during the final reading of the 1967 Abortion Bill:

In the whole of my public life I have never felt so badly about anything as I do about the Bill. As a human being who has fought to protect all that is best in mankind, and as one who respects the rights and dignity of all people, I protest vehemently against the Bill and all that it contains. Life is the most precious gift on earth. Man can take it away but he cannot give it back again. Life is man's most precious possession since if he loses it, he loses everything. He therefore has a right to life, which no one may take away from him. Man disregards this most fundamental right at his peril.

Let there be no doubt in anyone's mind as to how the Universal Declaration of Human Rights applied to the child. That representative body of all civilized peoples was proud to declare that mankind owes to the child the very best that it has to give. Without equivocation, it stated that by reason of his mental and physical immaturity, the child needs special legal protection before as well as after birth. The Bill makes a mockery of the Declaration of Human Rights and opens the door to an increasing disregard for the rights of the child.

It has never been shown that the foetus in the embryo stage is not alive. It has never been shown that at some time in advanced pregnancy the child suddenly becomes alive. The child, whether born or unborn, is not the chattel of its mother, to be treated according to her wishes and whims. This would be a travesty of motherhood. She is the first and greatest guardian of her child's safety and rights.

The child in the womb cannot, and must not be deprived of its life because his mother, or society, doesn't want him. Let me remind Parliament, if with the smug complacency of Englishmen it is anxious to forget, that we have had a Prime Minister and a Foreign Secretary who were the illegitimate children of servant girls.

It is true that a mother, or anyone else for that matter, has the right to have done for her whatever is necessary for her health, but not if it involves the killing of another person, whether unborn child or adult. What is supreme cannot be taken away because of what is partial. If a mother is psychologically disturbed through some other factors, whatever the cause, the unborn child is not responsible and cannot be punished as though he were.

Backstreet abortionists are rightly abhorred, but whatever the harm done to the woman, the first and greatest injustice is the taking of the child's life. The injustice is by no means abated by having the abortion carried out by doctors in the best aseptic conditions.

It is indeed our sacred duty to maintain the dignity and rights of mothers, but however deep our emotions at the sight of afflicted mothers, we will neglect at our peril the rights of the child ... the presentation of this bill is in itself an indictment of Parliament. The acceptance and support for the Bill is tantamount to a confession of failure to deal with the social maladies afflicting our society.

PETER MAHON
Sunday Telegraph, 1967

It is facile to argue that it was impossible to foresee how the 1967 Termination of Pregnancy Act would lead to abortion on demand. Its opponents predicted it at the time.

Sunday Telegraph, 5 January, 1997, Editor's Notebook

The baby with the cleft palate

In 2001 Dr Michael Cohn aborted a baby with a cleft palate at 28 weeks. That's a whole month after the legal limit for termination and two months after infants can survive outside the womb. The baby would have been very much alive and the procedure must have been horrible for the mother, medical staff and presumably the unborn baby …

The Abortion Act 1967 allows doctors to terminate a pregnancy after 24 weeks only if the baby would have a 'serious handicap'. What is a serious handicap? Who decides? Most cleft palates can be corrected by surgery. In the age of the makeover, are the imperfect not to be allowed into the world because they might let the side down?

ALLISON PEARSON
Evening Standard, 5 March, 2004

Infanticide is justifiable in some cases

Professor John Harris, a member of the British Medical Association's Ethics Committee, said 'It is well known that when a serious abnormality is not picked up, when you get a very seriously handicapped or indeed a very premature newborn … what effectively happens is that steps are taken not to sustain it on life support.

'There is a very widespread and accepted practice of infanticide in most countries. ... there is no obvious reason why one should think differently, from an ethical point of view, about a foetus when it is outside the womb rather than inside.'

The professor's comments were made during an unreported debate last week on sex selection, which was held as a part of the committee's consultation on human productive technologies. Professor Harris, who is also Professor of Bioethics at Manchester University, was asked what moral status he accorded an embryo and he endorsed infanticide in cases of a child carrying a genetic disorder that remained undetected during pregnancy.

He replied, 'I don't think infanticide is always unjustifiable. I don't think it is plausible to think that there is any change that occurs during the journey down the birth canal.' He declined to say up to what age he believed infanticide should be permissible. Professor Harris, who is one of the International Association of Bioethics and the author of fifteen books on the ethics of genetics, was condemned for his remarks.

Sunday Telegraph, 25 January, 2004

Prenatal diagnosis

This is morally licit if it respects the life and integrity of the embryo and the human foetus and is directed towards its safeguarding as an individual ... it is gravely opposed to the moral law when this is done with the thought of possibly inducing an abortion: a diagnosis must not be the equivalent of a death sentence.

CATECHISM OF THE CATHOLIC CHURCH

Down's Syndrome

In June 1995 Dominic Lawson became the father of Domenica, a
Down's Syndrome baby. At the beginning of the article quoted below
he described the elation that followed the birth and wondered how
anyone could argue against such children being given the chance of
life. He went on to dispute the moral grounds for aborting them:

Domenica's intellectual and physical progress will never be as
rapid or fluent as her sister's, and it will doubtless cost both
her and us enormous amounts of effort. But the point is, she
will continue to develop, however slowly, along the lines which
will reveal her to be a true mixture of the genes her parents
married in order to perpetuate.

And yet ... And yet a whole industry has been developed to
make it increasingly unlikely that children like Domenica Lawson
will be allowed to live. The National Health Service advises all
mothers-to-be over 35 to undergo medical procedures which
extract fluid from around the foetus, which is then subject to
chromosomal analysis. The NHS provides this service free
because the probability of Down's Syndrome – far and away
the commonest form of congenital mental handicap in the
population – appears to grow rapidly when the mother's age
increases beyond the mid-thirties.

But these procedures, either chorionic villus sampling or
amniocentesis, have significantly higher statistical risk of
causing miscarriage than the 36-year-old mother has of
carrying a Down's Syndrome baby. The chances of that woman
having a Down's baby, regardless of whether she has already
had such a child in the past, are about one in 300. But even
the less risky of the two procedures pressed on a middle-aged

woman by the NHS, (chorionic villus sampling) will, in about one case in a hundred, produce a spontaneous abortion.

According to Dr Miriam Stoppard's book *Pregnancy and Birth*, which is by no means hostile to these procedures, 'very occasionally CVS may lead to rupture of the amniotic sack, infection and bleeding. Even so, the procedure only seems to increase the risk of miscarriage by one per cent.' Even so? Only one per cent? It is amazing that these facts are meant to reassure us. There is method in this madness, however. The NHS will provide, gratis, an abortion, if their tests show that the mother is expecting a Down's Syndrome baby; an abortion even *well after the normal legal limit of 24 weeks* into the pregnancy, 'if there is a risk, that is, that if the child were born it would suffer such physical and or mental defects as to be seriously handicapped.'

This is nothing less than state-sponsored annihilation of viable, sentient human foetuses. In the People's Republic of China, the authorities wait until the children are born before starving them to death. In Hitler's Germany, even before the Final Solution to the Jewish problem, the Nazis were exterminating wholesale the mentally retarded. In this country the weeding-out process is done before birth, and only with the parent's consent. I do not think, however, that this constitutes a triumph for democracy. To the extent that this policy is more than half-baked eugenics, it is, to take the most charitable interpretation, based on the utilitarian idea that the child born with a physical or mental handicap will be an unhappy person, so unhappy that they will be better off dead. One needs only to state this proposition to see how presumptuous it is.

Not surprisingly I have, in the past week, been told by a number of well-meaning people, that 'they' – meaning children with Down's Syndrome – are 'particularly happy people'. I have no idea if this is true, and I am inherently suspicious of such generalizations. But I see no reason why Domenica should be an unhappier person than her older sister, despite the extra chromosome which she has in her every cell.

Yet one or two acquaintances have still asked us, 'Didn't you have the tests?' My wife says she thinks it will be very difficult to remain friends with such people. I think they are missing the point, although it is a very important point.

Of all the letters I have received since Domenica was born, perhaps the one which grasped this point best was from a fellow atheist who wrote, after approving our not 'having the tests':

'The reason why [such a decision] is admirable, of course, is that the sanctity of life is not just some obscure abstract principle. A life is a life, and every life can be filled with all kinds of positive things and real happiness – as I'm sure your daughter's will be.'

DOMINIC LAWSON
Spectator, June 1995

Chromosomic or genetic engineering

It is immoral to produce human embryos intended for exploitation as disposable genetic material. Certain attempts to *influence chromosonic or genetic inheritance* are not therapeutic but are aimed at producing human beings selected according to sex or other predetermined qualities. Such manipulations are contrary to the personal dignity of the human being and his integrity and identity which are unique and unrepeatable.

CATECHISM OF THE CATHOLIC CHURCH

Research on human embryos

The laws governing research on human embryos in Britain are among the most sophisticated in the world. Although tighter than in the United States, they are more liberal than most of Europe.

1. Cloning experiments involving human embryos are forbidden under the Human Fertilization and Embryology Act 1990. Certain other research on embryos is permitted under the Act following pioneering work by the Warnock Committee in 1994.

2. Clinics wanting to do research or offer treatment which involves keeping embryos out of the womb must obtain a licence from the Human and Embryology Authority.

3. Gene therapy – inserting genes into patients with inherited conditions such as cystic fibrosis – is permitted. Genetic manipulation of embryos to eliminate the condition from future generations, achieving a cure, is not. It is felt that too little is known about the long-term effects of altering an individual's genetic inheritance to allow such experiments.

The Times, March 1997

It is an illusion to claim moral neutrality in scientific research and its application.

CATECHISM OF THE CATHOLIC CHURCH

Pragmatism is like a warm bath which heats up so imperceptibly that you don't know when to scream.

BERTRAND RUSSELL
History of Western Philosophy

Prayer of Alcoholics Anonymous

Dear God, give us the serenity to face those things in life which we cannot change, and the courage to strive to change those things which should be changed, and in both to put our whole trust in Thee.

HOPE AND CONFIDENCE

Jesus said to His disciples:
Do not let your hearts be troubled.
Trust in God still, and trust in Me:
There are many rooms in my Father's house;
If there were not I would have told you.

JOHN 14. 1–5

I hope in the mercy of God who no one has ever taken for a
friend without being rewarded.

ST TERESA OF AVILA
E. Allison Peers, The Life of St Teresa of Avila

Hope is not based upon grace received, but upon the divine
onmipotence and mercy, by which even he who has not got
grace can obtain it, that he may reach eternal life. Anyone who
believes in God can be certain of the omnipotence of God *and*
His mercy.

ST THOMAS AQUINAS
Summa Theologica

Now God, who does nothing in vain, does not give us either strength or courage when we don't need them, but only when we do. He never fails us. Consequently we must always hope that He will help us if we entreat Him to do so. We should use these words of David:

'Why are you sad, my soul, and why do you trouble me? Hope in the Lord.'

ST FRANCIS DE SALES
Letters of Direction

Calm all the objections which might be taking shape in your mind and to which you need give no other answer than that you want to be faithful at all times, that you hope God will see to it that you are, without your trying to figure out whether He will or not; for such attempts are deceiving. We must not be afraid of fear; so much for that.

IBID.

The place God wants for us

For us, let it be enough to know ourselves to be in the place God wants for us (in the modern world) and carry on our work, even though it be no more than the work of an ant, infinitesimally small, and with unforeseeable results. Now is the hour of silent offering: therefore the hour of Hope. God alone, faceless, unfelt, yet undeniably God.

ABBÉ MONCHANIN
Ecrits Spirituels

Those in trouble

Let all those who are in trouble take this comfort to themselves, if they are trying to lead a spiritual life. If they call on God He will answer them. Though they have no earthly friend, they have Him, who, as He felt for His mother on the cross, now that He is in His glory, feels for the lowest and feeblest of His people.

CARDINAL NEWMAN
Meditations and Devotions

The book of Genesis fills me with great hope, when hope is in short supply; because one great man of God, the author of this book, looking back across the wastes of time, haunted by his own inadequacies, bored by the brutalities and banalities of everyday existence, still holds fast to paradise.

BISHOP STUART BLANCH

Now hope that is seen is not hope. For who hopes for what he sees? But if we hope for what we do not see, we wait for it with patience. Likewise the Spirit helps us in our weakness: for we do not know how to pray as we ought. We know that in everything God works for good with those who love Him; who are called according to His purpose.

ST PAUL TO THE ROMANS 8.24—9

GOD'S MERCY AND THE JUDGEMENT

The four last things: Heaven, Hell, Death and Judgement

Eschatology – the branch of theology which deals with the four last things and the final destiny of the soul and of humankind; a doctrine of belief about the second coming of God.

OXFORD ENGLISH DICTIONARY

What fear have you of the judgement? Would you like to be judged by me at the gates of Heaven? Would you feel confident that I should be lenient? Of course you would! Very well then! God will be more lenient still because he is better than me, and loves you (as is His right) in a still more lenient way ... you must feel nothing but confidence in the infinite mercy of God.

ABBÉ DE TOURVILLE
Letters of Direction

Judgement is whispering into the ear of a merciful and compassionate God the story of my life which I have never been able to tell.

CARDINAL HUME
To Be a Pilgrim

157

PURGATORY

All who die in God's grace and friendship, but still imperfectly purified, are indeed assured of their eternal salvation, but after death they undergo purification, so as to achieve the holiness necessary to enter the joy of heaven.

CATECHISM OF THE CATHOLIC CHURCH

It would be wrong to suppose that every soul has to undergo purification. We think of the millions in the world today who are deprived or oppressed – the undernourished, the victims of war and persecution. Their sufferings, humbly borne, surely amount in the eyes of God to 'worthy fruits of penance'. And this ... does not apply only to Christians, but even to 'those who, without blame on their part, have not yet arrived at an explicit knowledge of God, but who strive to lead a good life, thanks to His grace.'

VATICAN II
Lumen Gentium

As for certain lesser faults, we must believe that, before the Final Judgement, there is a purifying fire.

ST GREGORY

St Thérèse of Lisieux to another Carmelite, Sister Marie-Philomene,
who was afraid of purgatory:
Ma soeur Marie-Philomene, you have not enough trust, you are
too frightened of the good God. I assure you this distresses Him.
Don't fear purgatory because of the pain which is suffered
there, but wish not to go there in order to please God who
regrets so much this expiation.

General Gordon wrote this to a sister he particularly loved. His point
of view is strongly put but it is personal.
I have never felt the least doubt of our salvation. Nothing can be
more abject than the usual conception of God. Accept what I say
– namely – that He has put us in a painful position (I believe with
our perfect consent, for if Christ came to do His will, so did
we, His members) *to learn what He is and that He will extricate us.*
Imagine to yourself; what pleasure would it be to Him to burn
us or to torture us? Can we believe any *human being* capable of
creating us for such a purpose? Would it show His power? Why?'
He is omnipotent! Would it show His justice? He is righteous
– no one will deny it. We credit God with attributes which are
utterly hateful to the meanest of men. Looking at our darkness
of vision, how can He be what we credit Him with?

GENERAL GORDON OF KHARTOUM
Alan Moorehead, The White Nile

The Six Precepts of the Church
1. To hear Mass on Sundays, and all holidays of obligation.
2. To fast and abstain on the days commanded.
3. To confess our sins at least once a year.

4. To receive the Blessed Eucharist at least once a year.

5. To contribute to the support of our pastors.

6. Not to solemnize marriage at the forbidden times: nor to marry persons within the forbidden degree of kinship; nor clandestinely.

THE DAILY MISSAL

Feasts throughout the year

Festivals that are observed by the Catholics of England with an obligation of hearing Mass.

All Sundays in the year

January 1	The Circumcision of Our Lord
January 6	The Epiphany
June 29	SS Peter and Paul
August 13	The Assumption of Our Lady into heaven
November 1	All Saints
December 25	Christmas Day

Easter Sunday

Ascension Day (forty days after Easter)

Corpus Christi (Thursday after Trinity Sunday)

In Ireland besides the above:

March 17	St Patrick
December 8	The Immaculate Conception

In Scotland besides the above

March 19	St Joseph
December 8	The Immaculate Conception

IBID.

PETITION

Ask and it will be given to you; seek and you will find; knock and the door will be opened to you. For everyone who asks receives; he who seeks, finds; and to him who knocks, the door will be opened.

Which of you, if his son asks for bread, will give him a stone? Or if he asks for a fish, will give him a snake? If you then, though you are evil, know how to give good gifts to your children, how much more will your Father in Heaven give good gifts to those who ask him! So in everything, do to others what you would have them do to you, for this sums up the Law and the Prophets.

MATTHEW 7.7–12

Certain gifts God makes to the human soul without its asking or desiring; but there are other gifts which the grown-up soul, with the use of reason, can only have by its desire. We desire in general without knowing what to desire. We must pray to know how to pray ... Herod once said to a dancing girl, 'You may ask me for the half of my kingdom.' When we have ended our little dance of life, we are not offered half the Kingdom but all the Kingdom. The King has bidden us to ask.

VINCENT MCNABB
The Craft of Prayer

161

If prayer is regarded simply as a request to God to do what He would not do if we did not ask Him, and will do simply because we ask Him, we are wasting our time.

God is not a human being who gets up from point A and goes to point B and does something He has been asked. He is just present, and is love, through people who are in a right relationship with Him, and through them He does more than we ask or think.

ANON.

We are on surer ground when we simply lift up to God our needy condition than when we ask in detail for the things we need.

ST JOHN OF THE CROSS

INTERCESSION

A piece of work

Real intercession is not merely a petition but a piece of work,
involving perfectly costly surrender to God for the work He
wants done on other souls.

ANON.

Your prayer has always contributed

We must not picture destiny as a film unrolling for the most
part on its own but in which our prayers are sometimes allowed
to insert additional items. On the contrary; what the film
displays to us, as it unrolls already, are the results of our prayers
and of all our other acts. There is no question of *whether* an
event happened because of your prayer. When the event you
prayed for occurs your prayer has always contributed to it.
When the opposite event occurs your prayer has not been
ignored; it has been considered and refused, for your ultimate
good and the good of the whole universe.

C. S. LEWIS
Speaking of Prayer

O Marguerite, *ma soeur*, while I was rushing across land and sea, dedicated to the positive forces of the universe, passionately concerned with the sight of all the colours of the earth, you were lying immobile; silently, and in the secret depths of your being, changing the darkest shadows of the world into light. Tell me, in the eyes of the Creator, which of us had the better part?

TEILHARD DE CHARDIN
From the Preface to L'Energie Spirituelle by his sister Marguerite

The prayers of others

And the things that are not so ill with you and me as they might have been, is half owing to the number who lived faithfully a hidden life, and the rest in unmarked graves.

GEORGE ELIOT
Middlemarch

The goodness of God can only work by means of His creation. It uses even the degenerate and feeble. It can find a passage through every human absurdity and every corruption.

R. C. HUTCHINSON
A Child Possessed

God does not have favourites
Peter addressed Cornelius and his household:
'The truth I have now come to realize,' he said 'is that
God does not have favourites, but that anybody of
any nationality who fears God and does what is right,
is acceptable to Him.'

'It is true, God sent His Word to the people of Israel,
and it was to them that the good news of peace was
brought by Jesus Christ. But Jesus Christ is Lord of
all men.'

ACTS OF THE APOSTLES 10.34–38

A prayer of intercession

Remember us all, Lord, for good.

Have pity on us all, be reconciled with us all.

Fill our storehouses;

Preserve our marriages, nurture our children;

Lead forward our youth, sustain our old;

Comfort the weak-hearted, gather the scattered;

Restore the wanderers, and unite them to your Church.

Set free the troubled;

Voyage with the voyagers, travel with the travellers.

Protect the widow, shield the orphan;

Rescue the captive, heal the sick.

Remember, O Lord, all those who are on trial,

In exile, or in whatever affliction,

And remember all those who need your great mercy.

Remember those who love us, and those who hate us.

Remember all those who, through ignorance or forgetfulness we
    have forgotten.

Pour out your rich pity and save your people,
O Lord.

LANCELOT ANDREWES

Teachable

According to Sister Elisabeth of the Trinity, we are to make
ourselves enseignable, teachable. We are to be free within; our
souls are not to be cluttered up with noise and sterile activities,
but attentive and ready to detect the signs, sometimes so
delicate, of the presence of the Lord speaking to us.

A CARTHUSIAN MISCELLANY

DAILY PRAYER

Prayer is crucial to my daily life and I believe that all we have
to do to pray is to make space and time. Prayer is not something
we do: it is something God does if we allow Him to. I try to
give Him between half an hour and three-quarters of an hour
every day. If you include the Mass it is more, and the best time
of the day for me is early in the morning. I find it hard to use
the word prayer to 'lift up my mind and heart to God', as the
catechism said. So I just leave it to God and He takes care of it.
Most of the time I don't feel anything, no nice religious feelings,
no cosiness, no sense that I am 'giving God His due'. Maybe
that is what the Gospels mean when they talk about poverty of
spirit, and I am sure that everybody has a relationship with God
whether they know it or not.

I don't think I'm very good at prayer. I feel its a bit like my
jam-making. If I took my jam to a WI it wouldn't win. Imagine
a father working in his study and his two-year-old daughter
coming in while he is working: she is playing, running around
and all kinds of things. The important thing is that she has
come into his study to be with him. She can't be on his level
but she is saying 'I want to be with you'. That is how I feel
about my relationship with God. Going to Mass is a tangible
way of saying I want to be with God.

DELIA SMITH
Magazine article

Uselessness in prayer

The man or woman who prays regularly, day in day out, with absolutely nothing in the way of experience and with the feeling of uselessness much of the time, is often, perhaps always, growing in the life of the spirit more than another who finds delight in prayer.

ANON.

A prayer at morning

Cold, slow, silent, but returning, after so many hours.
The sight of something outside, the day is breaking.
May salt, this one day, be sharp upon my tongue,
May I sleep, this one night, without waking.

RANDALL JARRELL

The apologist's evening prayer

From all my lame defeats and Oh! much more,
From all the victories that I seem to score;
From cleverness shot forth on Thy behalf,
At which, while Angels weep, the audience laugh;
Thou, who wouldst give no sign, deliver me ...
From all my thoughts, even from my thoughts of Thee,
Oh thou, fair silence, fall and set me free.
Lord of the narrow gate and the needle's eye,
Take me from all my trumpery lest I die.

C. S. LEWIS

Moral decisions

Some rules apply in every case:

1. One may never do evil so that good may come of it.
2. The Golden Rule: 'Whatever you wish that men would do to you, do so to them' (Matthew).
3. Charity always proceeds by way of respect for one's neighbour and his conscience. 'Thus sinning against your brethren and wounding their conscience ... you sin against Christ' (Corinthians). Therefore 'it is right not to do ... anything that makes your brother stumble' (Romans).

CATECHISM OF THE CATHOLIC CHURCH

THE CONSCIENCE

Beware of trifling with your conscience. It is often said that second thoughts are best; so they are in matters of judgement, but not in matters of conscience. In matters of duty first thoughts are commonly better – they have more in them of the voice of God.

CARDINAL NEWMAN
Plain and Parochial Sermons

I have always contended that obedience, even to an erring conscience, was the way to gain light and that it mattered not where a man began so that he began on what came to hand and in faith.

CARDINAL NEWMAN
Apologia

Scruples and self-examination

O dear daughter, don't be examining yourself to see if what you are doing is little or much, good or bad, provided that it is not sinful and that in all good faith you are trying to do it for God. Do what you have to do ... think no more about it but turn your attention to what has to be done next.

ST FRANCIS DE SALES
Letters of Spiritual Direction

It is a great grace to practise self-examination; but too much is as bad as too little; believe me, by God's help, we shall advance more by contemplating the Divinity than by keeping our eyes fixed on ourselves.

ST TERESA OF AVILA

E. Allison Peers, The Life of St Teresa of Avila

The desire to have only good inclinations

Do not worry about your feelings, but act as if you had those which you would like to have. This is not done by making a mental effort, nor by seeking to feel that which you do not feel, but simply by doing without the feeling you have not got and behaving exactly as if you had it. When you realize that lack of feeling doesn't hinder reality, you will no longer put your trust in your own thoughts, but in that which our Lord makes you do. Come now! Have a little of that tranquil fearlessness which makes for good, without so much thought and scrupulousness. Behave just as naturally as if you were going down stairs!

The root of many of your troubles is the desire to have only good inclinations. That is neither necessary nor possible. In countless ways we shall always feel ourselves to be wicked, unstable and unreasonable. We must realize that this is our nature and not our real personality; not our true, deliberate and voluntary desires. Not the goal of our efforts.

ABBÉ DE TOURVILLE

Letters of Direction

On self-tormenting

My dear Child,

I am truly sorry to hear of your distress continuing, but I must put it to your own conscience, whether there is not in it somewhat of self-tormenting, and wilful peevishness, and whether the remedy is not, by God's mercy, in your own power. I must beg you to ask yourself whether you are really endeavouring to shake off the morbid feelings which haunt you as sincerely as you would endeavour to cure a toothache.

JOHN KEBLE
Letters of Spiritual Council

Do not keep accounts with Our Lord and say 'I did Him such an injury therefore He owes me such a grudge. He cannot be on good terms with me because I have not paid Him this and that; it would not be just otherwise.'

Go bankrupt! Let Our Lord love you without justice! Say frankly,'He loves me because I do not deserve it; and that is why I, in my turn, love Him as well as I can without worrying whether I deserve to be allowed to love Him.'

I know no other way of loving God. Therefore burn your account books! ... You will always offend God in some way; that is only one reason the more for making amends, both to yourself and to Him, by loving Him always and for ever more.

ABBÉ DE TOURVILLE
Letters of Direction

Religious depression

For it is impossible to derive consolation from our own feelings, because of their mutability: today we are well and our spiritual experience, partaking of these circumstances, is bright; but tomorrow some outward circumstances change – the sun does not shine, or the wind is chill and we are low, gloomy and sad. Then if our hopes were unreasonably high, they will now be depressed, and so our experience becomes flux and reflux, ebb and flow; like the sea, that emblem of instability.

F. W. ROBERTSON
Sermons on Religion and Life

Humiliation and the religious

There is a hunger for humiliation that is nothing else but a hunger for admiration turned inside out. It is a sincere desire to be despised, and it is perhaps a desire cherished only by those who might be saints. But is it not a desire to to be loved by angels only? And is it not a desire to despise what men admire? And do we not often despise what men admire in revenge for having to do without it?

THOMAS MERTON
The Sign of Jonas

On a Puritan family

I endeavoured in vain to give them more cheerful ideas of religion, to teach them that God is not a jealous, childish, merciless tyrant; that he is best served by a regular tenor of good actions – not by bad, ill-composed hymns and eternal apprehension. But the luxury of false religion is to be unhappy.

SYDNEY SMITH

173

Unworthiness

Sometimes we think we are unworthy of praying. This is a temptation. Every drop of water, from wherever it comes, is purified in evaporation; and so is every prayer ascending to God.

ST TERESA OF AVILA
E. Allison Peers, The Life of St Teresa of Avila

Often I dared not pray because of having offended His Majesty. But it is a most certain thing, that if we remember all the time that we are poor, and if our prayer is in His name, the people we love are given to us to be lifted up to God in intercessory love and affection.

IBID.

I used to find great consolation in reading about the lives of saints who had been sinners before the Lord brought then back to Himself.

IBID.

The blurred conscience

What made her so unusual was the absence of any moral problem. If I said to you 'I should never have thought that of a woman like you' I would be sure to hurt you to the quick. For Rosine there is no 'woman like you'. She never questions herself about her own behaviour.

SUZANNE CHANTAL
Le Coeur Battant

I was getting to a stage where I was not quite sure what sin was. I was in a kind of fog, drifting about without clues, and this is liable to happen when you go on and on doing something. It makes a confused sort of twilight in which everything is blurred, and the next thing you know you might be stealing or anything, because right and wrong have become things you do not look at, you are afraid to, and it seems better to live in a blur. Then comes the time when you wake up suddenly and the fog breaks, and right and wrong loom through it, sharp and clear like peaks of a rock, and you are on the wrong peak and know that unless you can manage to leave it now, you may be marooned there for life and ever after. Then as you don't leave it, the mist swirls round again, and hides the other peak, and you turn your back on it and try to forget it and succeed.

ROSE MACAULAY
The Towers of Trebizond

TEMPTATION

Temptation

I know what temptation consists of just as well as any priest.
To be tempted is to listen, when the conscience is asleep, to
the reasoning of the intelligence.

ANTOINE DE SAINT-EXUPÉRY
Vol de Nuit

God has decreed, and so it stands, that every man's undisciplined
spirit is his own punishment.

ST AUGUSTINE
The Confessions, Book 10

The imaginings of the flesh

Let them deal harshly with you who do not know with what
effort the truth is found and with what difficulty errors are
avoided; let them deal harshly with you who do not know how
rare and exacting it is to overcome the imaginings of the flesh
in the serenity of the intellect; let them deal harshly with you
who do not know with what pain the inner eye of man is
healed that he may glimpse his sun.

IBID.

THE WILL

Our part in the Mystical Body involves that continual use of the will which is called love.

DOM EUGENE BOYLAN

Ours is the age of the disordered will ... the attempt of the will to do the work of the imagination. Among the things that we try to will are happiness, creativity, love, sex and immortality.

W. B. YEATS
Letter to his son

Will and feeling

It is not easy to disentangle will and feeling: for in all intense will there is a strong element of emotion. Every volitional act has somewhere at the back of it a desire – and in all great and energising passions there is a pronounced volitional element. The 'synthesis of love and will' is hard to break down in practice. But I think we can say generally that the business of feeling is to inflame the will, to give it intention, gladness and vividness; to convert it from a dull determination into an eager, impassioned desire. It links up thoughts and action.

EVELYN UNDERHILL
Essentials of Mysticism

Against natural inclination

One little deed done against natural inclination for God's sake, though in itself of a conceding or passive character, to brook an insult, to face a danger, to resign an advantage, has in it a power outbalancing all the dust and chaff of mere profession.

CARDINAL NEWMAN
Fifteen Sermons Preached to Oxford University

SIN

Many sins are committed through pride but not all of
them happen proudly ... they happen so often by human
weakness; many are committed by men weeping and
groaning in their distress.

ST AUGUSTINE
On Nature and Grace

All sins are attempts to fill voids.

SIMONE WEIL
Gravity and Grace

I took hardly any notice of venial sins; and as to mortal sins,
although afraid of them, I was not so much as I ought to have
been; for I did not keep free from the danger of falling into
them. I can testify that this is one of the most grievous kinds of
life there is, for I had neither any joy in God nor any pleasure
in the world.

ST TERESA OF AVILA
E. Allison Peers, Life of St Teresa of Avila

Sins and their mirror opposites

Certain sins can manifest themselves as their mirror opposites which the sinner is able to persuade himself are virtues. Thus Gluttony can manifest itself as Daintiness, Lust as Prudery, Sloth as Senseless Industry, Envy as Hero Worship.

W. H. AUDEN
A Certain World

Mortal sin is a fundamental rejection of God's love.

For a sin to be mortal (meaning deathly):

1. It must be a serious matter, i.e. sleeping with another man's wife.
2. There must be sufficient reflection.
3. There must be full consent of the will.

Venial sin is a less serious rejection of the love of God. Venial means 'easily forgiven'. It is venial if:

1. The offence is not serious.
2. The person is not sufficiently aware of the evil involved.
3. Or does not fully consent to the sin.

Sins of whatever seriousness, do not have to be actions.

A person can sin by thought or by desire or by failing to do something that should be done.

A HANDBOOK FOR TODAY'S CATHOLICS

The six sins against the Holy Spirit
Despair
Presumption
Resisting the known truth
Envy of another's spiritual good
Obstinacy in sin
Final impenitence

THE ROMAN MISSAL

Two categories of men will achieve salvation; those who sin
and are strong enough to repent, and those who are too weak
ever to repent truly but are prepared, patiently and gratefully,
to bear all the weight of their sins; in their humility they are
acceptable to God.

AMBROSE OF OPTINA
Russian Staretz

Lately I have come to realize that my notion of sin has been
too limited. I thought of sin as a deliberate offence against
God, a partial or total rejection of Him. But now I see that it
is a mistake to restrict sin to specific acts ... Rather is sin to
be seen as an orientation, a more or less continual series of
choices against what one knows in one's heart to be right.

SISTER RUTH BURROWS
Before the Living God

Sin is sin whether it is committed by Pope, bishops, priests or lay people. The Pope goes to confession like the rest of us. I think of the Protestant churches as being composed of people who are good, and I don't mean this ironically. Most of the Protestants I know are good if narrow sometimes. But the Catholic Church is composed of those who accept what she teaches whether they are good or bad, and there is a constant struggle through the help of the sacraments to be good.

FLANNERY O'CONNOR

Sally Fitzgerald, The Letters of Flannery O'Conner

The weakness we condemn today in another, is the sin into which we will fall ourselves tomorrow unless God's grace preserves us.

ST JOHN OF THE CROSS

PENANCE

In the thirteenth century St Thomas Aquinas firmly attested that penance is 'medicinal', *not* vindictive. God does not 'punish' us for our sins but offers us corrective suffering which can purify our love for Him.

God softens the sinner's heart so that he can repent; such repentance then alters his situation since guilt is forgiven and eternal condemnation is no longer due.

RICHARD DE ST VICTOR
Twelfth-century theologian

Thou knowest this man's fall but thou knowest not his wrastling which perchance, was such that his very fall was acceptable to God.

DOROTHEUS

On sadness
I say that even if we felt we might have neither the strength nor the courage to resist temptation should it befall us, so long as we desired to resist it and hoped that if it did come our way God would rescue us, then we must not be sad.

Neither do we always have to feel strong and courageous; it is enough that we hope that we will have the strength and courage when and where we need them. We don't have to have a sign that these virtues will be ours; it is enough if we hope that God will help us.

Now God, who does nothing in vain, does not give us either strength or courage when we don't need them but only when we do. He never fails us. Consequently we must always hope that He will help us if we entreat Him to do so.

ST FRANCIS DE SALES
Letters of Spiritual Direction

The Evil One is well-pleased with sadness and melancholy.

IBID.

THE DOCTRINE OF HELL

As the weeds are pulled up and burned in the fire, so it will be at the end of the age. The Son of Man will send out his angels, and they will weed out of his kingdom everything that causes sin and all who do evil. They will be thrown into the fiery furnace, where there will be weeping and gnashing of teeth.

MATTHEW 13.40

I tell you my friends, do not be afraid of those who kill the body and after that can do no more. But I will show you whom you should fear. Fear him who, after killing the body, has power to throw you into hell. Yes, I tell you, fear him.

LUKE 12.4

Jesus often speaks of 'Gehenna', of the unquenchable fire reserved for those who, to the end of their lives, refuse to believe and be converted, where both body and soul can be lost.

CATECHISM OF THE CATHOLIC CHURCH

More than twenty of Christ's sayings in the Gospels refer in unambiguous terms to the doctrine of hell. We cannot therefore reject the belief in hell without throwing doubt on every saying of our Lord, with the result that the Gospels can no longer be accepted as a divinely inspired guide to life. If on the other hand we accept the record of our Lord's teaching on eternal punishment as correct, and nonetheless reject that teaching, we must also reject the belief that Jesus was both God and Man, for God cannot deceive us and a fallible God is a contradiction in terms.

ARNOLD LUNN
Popular Christianity

If you discount the idea of eternal punishment and so rob Christianity of its sharp issues and severe outlines, you alter its character radically; it is no longer the same religion.

FATHER RONALD KNOX

In the long run the answer to all those who object to the doctrine of hell is itself a question: 'What are you asking God do?' To wipe out men's past sins and at all costs to give them a fresh start, smoothing every difficulty and offering every miraculous help? But He has done so, on Calvary. To forgive them? They refuse to be forgiven. To leave them alone? Alas, I am afraid that is what He does.

C. S. LEWIS
The Problem of Pain

Freud has unfortunately overlooked the fact that man has never
yet been able to hold his own against the powers of darkness —
that is, of the unconscious. Man has always stood in need of the
spiritual help which each individual's own religion held out
to him. The opening up of the unconscious always means the
outbreak of intense spiritual suffering; it is as when a flourishing
civilization is abandoned to invading hordes of barbarians, or
when fertile fields are exposed by the bursting of a dam to a
raging torrent.

CARL JUNG
Modern Man in Search of a Soul

Do not get heated

Do not get heated because of the wicked;
do not be jealous of the perpetrators of sin;
for, like the grass they quickly wither,
like fresh green grass they wilt.

Trust in the Lord and do good,
settle down in the land and make faithfulness your friend,
and take great delight in the Lord;
rely on Him and He will act,
and He will bring forth like daylight your righteousness,
and your right like the moon.

Be silent towards the Lord
and supplicate Him;
do not get heated because of anyone who makes
                                 his way succeed,
or who pulls off his schemes.

187

Refrain from anger, leave wrath alone.
Do not get heated – it would be for nothing but harm.
For the wicked will be cut off,
and those who wait for the Lord,
they are the ones who will inherit the land.
Just a little while and the wicked man does not exist.

PSALM 37

Crosses

Just because a cross is a cross, does it follow that it is the cross
    God intended for us?
Just because a job is a nuisance, does it mean it is therefore
    good for you?

THOMAS MERTON
Monica Furlong, Merton: A Biography

Charity

To expect too much from life is to have a sentimental view of
life. Charity is hard and endures.

FLANNERY O'CONNOR
The letters of Flannery O'Connor, edited by Sally Fitzgerald

Ode to midwinter

Study me then, you who shall lovers be,
At the next world, that is at the next spring,
For I am every dead thing,
In whom love wrought new alchemie.
For his art did expresse
A quintessence even from nothingnesse,
He ruined me and I am rebegot
Of Absense, Darknesse, Death; things which are not.

JOHN DONNE

All which I took from thee
Not for thy harms,
But just that thou might'st seek it in my arms.
All which thy child's mistake
Fancies as lost, I have stored for thee at home:
Rise, clasp my hand and come.

FRANCIS THOMPSON
The Hound of Heaven

'Indeed the times are troubled,' he said, 'But we must
remember that we are in God's hands.'
'I know we are,' said Mrs Brandon earnestly, laying her hand
on the Vicar's sleeve, 'and that is what is so very dreadful'.

ANGELA THIRKELL
The Brandons

The shell
If thou couldst empty all thyself of self,
Like to a shell dishabited,
Then might He find thee on an ocean shelf,
And fill thee with Himself instead.
But thou art so replete with very thou,
And hast such shrewd activity,
That when He comes He'll say, 'It is enough
                Unto itself – t'were better let it be:
It is so small and full,
And has no need of me.'

T. E. BROWN

DIFFICULTIES IN PRAYING

I never have the satisfaction of feeling I have prayed, nor even the certainty that I have been faithful. I have no certainties at all about myself except that I am loved by God and God's love can be relied upon to purify, transform me and finally complete the work.

SISTER RUTH BURROWS

Living in Mystery

Our yearning for reassurance

Our methods, the scaffolding we use to support ourselves, must never be confused with prayer itself or given much importance. That this is a common error hardly needs mentioning. It lies behind all our confusions and anxieties regarding prayer, our yearning for reassurance, for someone to teach us how to get it right. It lies behind the complaints: 'I cannot pray', 'My prayer is hopeless'. It is the source of all discouragement. Our attention is on ourselves. We are centre-stage and our entertainment of God is what matters and what a mess we are making of it! How, oh, how can we improve our performance?

Inevitably, we feel badly about ourselves: miserable, unspiritual. It is quite impossible that God would be interested in such as us. We must do something about improving ourselves before we can risk exposing ourselves to God ... The irony of it! For us the Holy Spirit is not around. If we bear in mind the essence of prayer and confront our difficulties we shall see that these have nothing to do with prayer, but only with our false expectations and lack of faith. What Divine Love wants us to do is to take our eyes off ourselves and fix them on Jesus, and spread out our anxieties beneath his gaze.

IBID.

Long prayers

God is not the more pleased with prayers, merely because they are long, nor are Christians the more edified. It is much better to make up by the frequency of our devotions what we lack in the length of them, when we feel our spirits dry, and our hearts straightened. We may also cry to God for the aids of His own Holy Spirit, even in the middle of our prayer, to carry us forward in that work: but every man is not fit to pray long. God has bestowed a variety of natural as well as spiritual gifts upon men; nor is the best Christian, or a saint with the greatest gifts, fit for long prayers.

ISAAC WATTS

A Guide to Prayer

I never dared pray without a book

During eighteen years I never began to pray without a book. It was not usual for me to suffer from aridity and this only happened when I had no book, where upon my soul at once became disturbed and my thoughts began to wander.

ST TERESA OF AVILA

E. Allison Peers, Life of Saint Teresa of Avila

Distractions

... and very often over a period of years I was more occupied
in wishing my hour of prayer was over, and in listening
whenever the clock struck, than in thinking of the things
that were good. Again and again I would rather have done
any penance that might have been given me, than practise
recollection as a preliminary to prayer. It is a fact that either
through the intolerable power of the devil's assaults, or through
my own bad habits, I did not immediately betake myself to
prayer. In the end the Lord would come to my help. Afterwards,
when I had forced myself to pray, I would find that I had more
tranquillity and happiness than at certain other times when I had
prayed because I wanted to.

IBID.

Men give me an answer

Lord God, I don't wonder that my prayers fall short of you,
even I myself fail to pay the least attention to what I'm praying
about. So often I consider my as prayer as just a job I have to
do, a duty to be performed. I 'get it out of the way' and then
relax, glad to have it behind me.

And yet, my God, I feel it hard to be sorry for praying so
poorly. How can a man hope to speak with You? You are so
distant and so mysterious ... Lord, to pray my whole life long
without hearing an answer, isn't that too much to ask? You see
how I run away from you time and time again, to speak with
men who give me an answer, to busy myself with things that
give me some kind of response. You see how much I need to
be answered. And yet my prayers never receive a word of

reply. Or should I say that ... the occasional light I receive in
meditation is Your word, Your enlightenment? This, of course,
is the pat and ready answer which pious writers are so eager
to give. But I find it very hard to believe. Again and again I find
only myself in all these experiences, only the empty echo of
my own cry, when it's You Yourself that I want to hear.

KARL RAHNER
Encounters With Silence

For the noise of a fly

I throw myself down in my chamber, and I call in and invite
God and His angels thither, and when they are there,
neglect God and His angels, for the noise of a fly, for the
rattling of a coach, for the whining of a door.

JOHN DONNE
At the Funeral of Sir William Cockayne

Stone-cold

Surely our prayers are sometimes so luke-warm, stone-cold
indeed, and hardly prayers at all: they are so distant in our
thought that we do not even notice this fact with pain – for if
we were even to feel the pain we should be praying again.

ST AUGUSTINE

Feminism

The message, whether explicit or tacit, that the Chorus of
Western Women addresses to the Chorus of Men, in this
twilight of our millenium, goes like this: 'I can cook once for
a party, once to express myself, once to pass on a tradition,
once out of necessity, and once for love, but I will not cook
three hundred and sixty-five days a year just because it has
been decided that my role is that of cooking and yours that of
sitting down to eat.' Something fundamental has changed in the
collective consciousness, but since almost nothing has changed
when it comes to our actual habits, the result is a constant
cloud of discontent. The man, however big a contribution he
may make to the family budget, is seen as a parasite if he fails
to contribute to the housework. Perhaps we will see a new
modus vivendi, a redistribution of roles, or perhaps no system of
compensation is possible now ...

If I can't cook it's because I'm not worthy to cook ... as the
unworthy alchemist can never obtain gold nor the unworthy
knight win the joust. Even my attempts to pitch in are frowned
upon, seen not as a demonstration of goodwill but as a hypocrisy,
a smokescreen, a histrionic exhibition. I cannot save myself by
Works, but only by the Grace which has not and will not be
conceded. If I manage to cook an omelette, it is not the first
step towards progress and interior growth: no, because there's
no way that's a Real Omelette, its a forger's hoax, a charlatan's
trick. Cooking is God's trial, something I have failed once and
for all, undeserving of initiation. All I can do is to seek out other
ways to justify my presence on this earth.

ITALO CALVINO
The Road to San Giovanni

St Helena's prayer to the Magi

Your gifts were not needed.

Like me you were late in coming ... The shepherds were here long before; they had joined the chorus of angels before you were on your way. For you the primordial discipline of the heavens was relaxed and a new defiant light blazed among the disconcerted stars.

How laboriously you came, taking sights and calculating, when the shepherds had run barefoot! How odd you looked on the road, attended with what outlandish liveries, laden with such preposterous gifts!

You came at length to the final stages of your pilgrimage and the great stars still stood above you. What did you do? You stopped to call on King Herod. Deadly exchanges of mobs and magistrates against the innocent!

Yet you came and were not turned away. You too found room before the manger. Your gifts were not needed, but they were accepted and put carefully away. In that new order of charity that had just come to life there was room for you too. You were not lower in the eyes of the Holy Family than the ox and the ass.

You are my especial patrons, and patrons of all latecomers, of all who are infused with knowledge and speculation, of all who stand in danger by reason of their talents.

Dear cousins, pray for my poor overloaded son. May he too, before the end, find kneeling space in the straw. Pray for the great lest they perish utterly ...

For His sake, who did not reject your curious gifts, pray always for the learned, the oblique, the delicate. Let them not

be quite forgotten at the throne of God when the simple come
into their kingdom.

EVELYN WAUGH

St Helena and the True Cross

St Helena was the mother of the first Christian emperor, Constantine.

A carol

Beyond this room
Daylight is brief.
Frost with no harm
Burns in white flame
The green holly leaf.
Cold on the wind's arm
Is ermine of snow.

Child with the sad name,
Your time is come
Quiet as moss.
Your journey now
For our belief,
Between the rich womb
And the poor cross.

JILL WHISTLER

Initials in the Heart by Lawrence Whistler

PEACE

Peace I leave you, my peace I give you. I do not give you as the world gives. Do not let your hearts be troubled, and do not be afraid.

JOHN 14.27

Note well. It is when he is being given up to the cross that he gives us 'his peace'. Thus it is not an absence of suffering and struggle. It is something more profound. It is peace of the heart.

CARTHUSIAN NOVICE CONFERENCES

Rejoice in the Lord always; again I say rejoice. Let your gentleness be known to everyone. The Lord is near. Do not worry about anything, but in everything by prayer and supplication with thanksgiving let your requests be made know to God. May the peace of God which passeth all understanding guard your hearts and your minds in Christ Jesus.

ST PAUL TO THE PHILIPPIANS 4.4—7

A certain lightheartedness

We cannot be peaceful if we are restless, full of anxieties,
sins, weaknesses, the future, friends, everything. By contrast,
the gospel invites us to have a certain lightheartedness,
a lightheartedness quite properly scandalous in the eyes of
practical people, sufficient unto themselves, accustomed to
anticipating the future, planning for every eventuality.

CARTHUSIAN NOVICE CONFERENCES

My soul there is a countrie

My soul there is a countrie
Afar beyond the stars,
Where stands the winged sentrie
All skillful in the wars.
There above noise and danger
Sweet peace sits crown'd with smiles,
And one born in a manger
Commands the beauteous files.
He is thy gracious friend,
And (O my soul awake)
Did in pure love descend
To die here for thy sake.
If thou canst get but thither,
There grows the flower of peace,
The Rose that cannot wither
Thy fortresse and thy ease.
Leave then thy foolish ranges:
For none can thee secure
But one who never changes
Thy God, thy Life, thy Cure.

HENRY VAUGHAN

Pax

All that matters is to be one with the living God
to be a creature in the house of the God of Life.

Like a cat asleep on a chair.
at peace, in peace
and at one with the master of the house, with the mistress,
at home, at home in the house of the living,
sleeping on the hearth, and yawning before the fire.

Sleeping on the hearth of the living world
yawning at home before the fire of life
feeling the presence of the living God
like a great reassurance,
a deep calm in the heart,
a presence
as of a master sitting at the board
in his own and greater being,
in the house of life.

D. H. LAWRENCE

Innisfallen

I know of no more perfect place than Innisfallen to spend a
summer's day. It is a country in miniature: it has its valleys, its
green pastures and its dark woods, its creeks and its bays.
There is a holy peace over it, and a man parting the thick bushes
comes on the old grey ruin almost fearfully, thinking as he
stands before the altar, whose cloth is a green moss, that if a

saint wished to show himself to men, this is the place where
he might shine a moment, his sandals deep in summer flowers.

H. V. MORTON
The Magic of Ireland

Sweet chance that led my steps abroad
Beyond the town, where wild flowers grow,
A rainbow and a cuckoo, Lord!
How rich and great the times are now!
Know all ye sheep
And cows that keep
On staring that I stand so long
In grass that's wet from heavy rain
A rainbow and a cuckoo's song
May never come together again.
May never come this side the tomb.

W. H. DAVIES

The donkey

When fishes flew and forests walked
  And fig grew upon thorn,
Some moment when the moon was blood
  Then surely I was born.

With monstrous head and sickening cry
  And ears like errant wings,
The devil's walking parody
  Of all four footed things.
The tatter'd outlaw of the earth
  Of ancient crooked will!
Starve me, scourge, deride me,
  I am dumb,
I keep my secret still.

Fools, for I also had my hour,
  One far fierce hour and sweet,
There was a shout about my ears,
  And palms were at my feet.

G. K. CHESTERTON

Animals

How strange that God brings us into such intimate contact with
creatures of whose real destiny we remain forever ignorant.

C. S. LEWIS

Put into the world to serve men

Those who were attached to animals were in the majority in
Forty Hill and they could not imagine a future life in which
they would be separated from their horses, their dogs, their
cats ... My mother believed that domestic animals, 'put into
the world to serve men' were immortal, but that all the rest
lived and died and that was the end of them. She was opposed
by Mrs Thresher and several supporters who argued that you
had to draw the line somewhere. If dogs, why not rats? Why
not jellyfish? Why not tapeworms? Why not the most primitive
of all forms of life manifesting themselves in a single cell?
Long and earnest discussions took place, but in the end my
mother was victorious, agreement was reached and pets were
confirmed in their possession of souls.

NORMAN LEWIS
Jackdaw Cake

Pleasure and play

Thanks to the wonderful bounty of Christianity, the whole of
our 2,000-year culture is the setting of the world free for play,
for spiritual pleasure, for the free imitation of Christ.

OSIP MANDELSTAM
Nadezhda Mandelstam, Hope against Hope

Extraordinarily happy

A sense of how extraordinarily happy I have been, of enormous
gratitude to my Creator, overwhelms me often. I believe with
a passionate, unshakeable conviction that, in all circumstances
and at all times, life is a blessed gift; that the spirit which
animates it is one of love and not hate or indifference, of
creativity not destruction, of order not chaos.

MALCOLM MUGGERIDGE
Radio interview

And life itself is only an instant,
Only the dissolving of ourselves in all others,
As though in gift to them;
Only a wedding, bursting in
   through the window from the street,
Only a song, a dream, a grey blue pigeon.

ATTRIBUTED TO BORIS PASTERNAK
The Wedding Party

Ella cantava e il puro canto rendeva
Puro tutte le cose.

When she sang, her pure song
Made everything pure.

GABRIELLE D'ANNUNZIO
L'Innocente

Under a Wiltshire apple tree
Some folk as can afford,
So I've heard say,
Set up a sort of cross
Right in the garden way
To mind 'em of the Lord.

But I, when I do see
Thik apple tree
An' stoopin' limb
All spread wi' moss,
I think of Him
And how He talks wi' me.

I think of God
And how He trod
That garden long ago,
He walked, I reckon, to and fro
And then sat down
Upon the groun'
Or on some limb
What suited Him
Such as you see
On many a tree,
And on thik very one
Where I at set o' sun
Do sit and talk Wi' He.

And mornings too, I rise and come
An' sit down where the branch be low,
And bird do sing, a bee do hum,
The flowers in the border blow,
And all my hearts so glad and clear
As ponds where mists do disappear
As pools a-laughing in the light
When morning air is swep' an' bright
As pools what got all Heaven in sight
So's my heart's cheer
When He be near.

He never pushed the garden door,
He left no footprint on the floor;
I never heard 'Un stir nor tread
And yet His Hand do bless my head,
And when 'tis time for work to start
I take Him with me in my heart.

And when I die, pray God I see
At very last thik apple tree
An' stoopin' limb,
And think of Him
And all He been to me.

ANNA BUNSTON

GRACE

What is grace?

Grace is a supernatural gift of God, freely bestowed on us for our sanctification and salvation.

Grace is favour, *the free and undeserved help* that God gives us to respond to His call to become children of God, adoptive sons, partakers of the divine nature and of eternal life.

Grace is a *participation in the life of God* ... by Baptism the Christian participates in the grace of Christ, the Head of His body. As an adopted son he can henceforth call God 'Father' in union with the only Son.

The vocation to eternal life is *supernatural*. It depends entirely on God's gratuitous initiative, for He alone can reveal and give Himself. It surpasses the power of the human intellect and will, as that of every other creature.

The grace of Christ is the free gift that God makes to us of His own life, infused by the Holy Spirit into our soul to heal it of sin and sanctify it. It is the *sanctifying grace or deifying grace* received in Baptism. It is in us the source of the work of sanctification.

CATECHISM OF THE CATHOLIC CHURCH

Habitual grace and actual grace

Habitual grace (is) the permanent disposition to live and act in keeping with God's will. It is distinguished from actual graces which refer to God's interventions, whether at the beginning of conversion or in the course of the work of sanctification.

God's free initiative demands *man's free response*, for God has created man in His image by conferring on Him, along with free will, the power to know Him and to love Him ... He has placed in man a longing for truth and goodness that only He can satisfy.

IBID.

Supernatural grace

... Grace also includes the gifts that the Spirit grants us to associate us with His work ... there are sacramental graces, gifts proper to the different sacraments.

Since it belongs to the supernatural order, grace escapes our experience and cannot be known except by faith. We cannot therefore rely on our feelings or our works to conclude that we are justified and saved. However, reflection on God's blessings in our life and in the lives of the saints offers us a guarantee that grace is at work in us too and spurs us on to an ever greater faith and an attitude of trustful poverty.

A pleasing illustration of this attitude is found in the reply of Joan of Arc to a question posed as a trap by her ecclesiastical judges: asked if she knew that she was in God's grace, she replied: 'If I am not, may it please God to put me in it; if I am, may it please God to keep me there.'

IBID.

We would become proud

Most of us are not strong enough for God to inundate us with manifest grace. We would become proud and claim it as our own; we would grasp the gifts instead of yielding to the Giver; we would lose the invaluable means of pure faith.

And who knows? The light of grace is so translucent and delicate that its presence in all its purity remains hidden, often unperceived. It is only when it passes through our sensibility that it becomes visible.

CARTHUSIAN NOVICE CONFERENCES

All human nature vigorously resists grace because grace changes us and the change is painful.

FLANNERY O'CONNOR
The Letters of Flannery O'Connor, edited by Sally Fitzgerald

You have to practise self-discipline

It's true that grace is the free gift of God but in order to put yourself in the way of being receptive to it, you have to practise self-discipline.

IBID.

To do what He has bid

You have to seek His face; obedience is the only way of seeking Him. If you are to believe the truths He has revealed, to regulate yourselves by His Precepts ... to adhere to His church and people, why is it except that He has bid you? And to do what He bids is to obey Him. And to obey Him is to approach Him – an approach to Him who is not far off, though He seems so, but close behind this visible scheme of things which hides Him from us.

CARDINAL NEWMAN

The Seven Sacraments

1. BAPTISM: By which we are made Christians, children of God, members of His Holy Church, and heirs to eternal life.

2. CONFIRMATION: By which we receive the Holy Spirit to make us strong and perfect Christians, and soldiers of Christ.

3. THE HOLY EUCHARIST: Which is really, truly and substantially the Body and Blood, the Soul and Divinity, of Jesus Christ, under the appearances of bread and wine. The Holy Eucharist is not only a Sacrament, in which we receive our divine Lord for the food and nourishment of our souls, and in which He is really present to be adored; it is also a Sacrifice, the Sacrifice of the Holy Mass, in which, at the time of consecration, the bread and wine are changed into the Body and Blood of Jesus Christ, and in which He is offered up for us to His eternal Father.

4. RECONCILIATION: By which the sins committed after baptism are forgiven.

5. ANOINTING OF THE SICK: Which, in dangerous illness, and in preparation for death, comforts the soul, remits sin, and restores health if God sees this to be expedient.

6. HOLY ORDERS: By which bishops, priests and other ministers of the Church receive power and grace to perform their sacred duties.

7. MATRIMONY: Which is the Sacrament of Christian Marriage.

After Communion

Why should I call thee Lord, who art my God?
  Why should I call thee friend, who art my love?
Or King, who art my very spouse above?
Or call thy sceptre on my heart thy rod?
  Lo, now thy banner over me is love.
All heaven flies open to me at thy nod:
For thou hast lit thy flame in me, a clod.
  Made me a nest for dwelling of thy Dove.
  What wilt thou call me in our home above,
Who now hast called me friend? How will it be
  When thou for good wine settest forth the best?
Now thou dost bid me come and sup with thee,
  Now Thou dost make me lean upon Thy breast:
How will it be with me in time of Love?

CHRISTINA ROSSETTI

Fasting and abstinence

1. The age when abstinence becomes binding is fourteen.
2. The obligation to fast is from the age of eighteen to the age of sixty.
3. Fasting and abstinence (doing without meat, for instance) are binding throughout the Church on Ash Wednesday and Good Friday only.
4. On Fridays (in union with the suffering and death of Our Lord) we are to practise some sort of self-denial – usually eating fish – but it is left to the free choice of the individual.

A HANDBOOK FOR TODAY'S CATHOLICS

The Eucharistic fast

1. Water and medicine may be taken at any time.
2. Solid food and drinks may be taken up to one hour before Holy Communion.
3. Those who are old or who suffer from any infirmity, as well as those who take care of them, can receive Holy Communion even if they have eaten something in the last hour.

IBID.

The Eucharist

You remember Christ's words over the bread: 'This is my Body'. They are simple words, words that could not be simpler. There is a subject, a verb of affirmation and a complement.

If we now turn to the discourse on the bread of life recorded by Saint John, we cannot help being struck by the force and realism used by Jesus there too. It is one of His most remarkable discourses.

In it Christ offers Himself to mankind as food, as bread come down from heaven, as the bread given by God Himself. At the outset, we understand Christ to be the bread of life because He is the Word of God: He feeds us with His truth and with His teaching. But by an imperceptible transition, Jesus then passes on to the Eucharist. And here His discourse takes on a near shocking realism: 'He who eats my flesh and drinks my blood has eternal life' (John 6.53). And He repeats the same statement several times, as though afraid of not being understood – so often that the listening Jews were horrified. To understand their sense of outrage and how at the same time their sense of outrage underlines the objective, realistic character of the Lord's words, we have to put ourselves in those Jews' places as they listened to Him talking about eating the flesh of the Son of Man, and above all drinking His blood.

For people who had been brought up from childhood to think of drinking blood as something absolutely forbidden and abominable, their reaction on hearing Jesus' words was physical nausea. They were appalled, and we can see why. 'This is intolerable language! How could anyone accept it' (John 6.60). They left Jesus and went away. But, we observe, Jesus did not retract one word of what He had been saying; and the Jews understood Him perfectly. All He said to the apostles was: 'What about you, do you want to go away too?' And then it was that Simon Peter made his famous reply: 'Lord, who should we go to? You have the message of eternal life.' (John 6.67).

Furthermore, this is the sense in which Christians interpreted the words in earliest times. 'Anyone who eats the bread or drinks the wine unworthily will be behaving unworthily towards the body and blood of the Lord' (Corinthians 11.27)

According to the Christian faith, Christ's body is really – I do not say physically – present in the bread, and His blood is really present in the wine. We have, at once, to believe in this presence and also to believe this presence is not like other presences. There is no word to express it, since there is no other example of this mode of presence in nature. The mode may be called spiritual, but it is none the less as real as, if not more real than, the presence of a being of flesh and blood. And Christ Himself suggests as much, without modifying any of the brutal realism of His discourse, by concluding with the words: 'The spirit is what gives life, the flesh has nothing to offer' (John 6.63).

The moment, of course, that we try to imagine what the Eucharistic presence of Christ actually is, we find ourselves in a maze of explanations which would require a theological training to unravel. And it is only fair to admit that theology has succeeded in making this mode of presence intelligible at least to some degree, or at least in demonstrating what it is not.

It is hard to steer a course between interpretations tending on the one hand to physical realism, and on the other to pure symbolism: both tendencies are equally wrong. Physical realism (as) an interpretation is ... perfectly legitimate, provided always that we merely regard it as a way of representing the reality of the presence, while knowing all the while that the presence is of a totally different order. Christ is in no sense "shut up" in the host or in the tabernacle.

This truly real presence is called sacramental. The mode of presence, as we have already said, is unique: a supernatural and divine presence of Christ's humanity. Thus, it is neither purely symbolic nor purely physical. Jesus is not in the bread and wine as in a place. When we eat the consecrated bread we do not physically touch the Body of Christ. No one who tries too precisely will ever succeed in producing a true definition. The Eucharist is still unchanged, for all the explanation, and will remain so until the end of time.

And it all depends what we mean by presence when we enter the realm of philosophy and find ourselves obliged to use technical terms, as in all forms of science. Thus, philosophically speaking, presence is an analogical concept, by which we mean that there are a number of ways of being present. I am present to you because I am only sitting a few feet way from you ... You may pick up the telephone and speak to a friend: again, you are present to him, despite the physical distance, in yet another way.

So the modes of presence are very varied. When we say that Christ is really present in the Eucharist, we mean to convey that a link of presence has been set up between the bread and wine on the one hand, and the Body and Blood of Christ on the other. Christ is now living in the glory of the Father – a non-terrestrial life – and hence His presence can never take a terrestrial form. Each and every one of the hosts consecrated throughout the world is related to the presence of Christ, without Christ being either changed or multiplied.

And now to speak of the Eucharist as sacrifice – since this was above all the reason why Christ instituted it, we are brought into relationship with the sacrifice on the Cross … we proclaim His passion; and by Communion we are united to the sacrifice of Christ and share its fruits.

I have already mentioned that the Christian life consists in reliving the mystery of Christ. But by the same token, we have also to relive His passion and His death on the Cross, and this is what gives an almost infinite dimension to our sufferings, our troubles, as well as the quality of participating, in the name of mankind, in all suffering. One of the fruits of the Eucharistic sacrifice should be precisely this: to help us to live this particular truth.

The Eucharistic sacrifice is also the pre-eminent sacrifice of praise. For Christ's offering of Himself is now consummated in the eternal glory of God, and of this praise the offering of the Eucharist is the highest form. We too have a part in this praise.

We ought to regard the Eucharist as an inestimable treasure. How amazing it is, once you start thinking about it! The Church could have got rid of the Eucharist centuries ago! Considering all the heresies, all the attacks, all the minimizirg interpretations of which the Eucharist has been the object it would have sufficed to cease celebrating it, or to cease consecrating priests, and that would have been the end of it. Yet Christians of all traditions despite the strife, despite the clash of doctrine, have always retained the Eucharistic celebration. People may argue about it, but it is always there, an irrefutable and abiding sign of the Son of Man's incomprehensible love for His fellow men.

RENÉ VOILLAUME
Faith and Contemplation

Our Lord has taken the lowest place in such a way that no one can take it from Him.

ABBÉ HUVELIN

Marriage

For there is nothing better and more precious than when two of one heart and mind keep house together ... but then they know it best themselves.

HOMER
Odyssey, Odysseus to Nausicaa

No trap so mischievous to the field preacher as wedlock, and it is laid on him at every hedge corner. Matrimony has quite maimed poor Charles (Wesley) and might have spoiled John (Wesley) and George Whitefield, if a wise Maker had not graciously sent them a pair of ferrets.

Dear George has now got his liberty again and he will escape well if he is not caught by another tenterhook. Eight or nine

215

years ago, having been grievously tormented with housekeepers, I truly thought about looking out for a Jezebel myself.

BISHOP ERRIDGE OF EVERTON

The pace of a hen
It distresses me that we have so little confidence in God, and so much love for ourselves. When we have made little spiritual progress, the smallest things will trouble us. Yet we presume to think ourselves spiritual. Now to me it seems that this sort of life is an attempt to reconcile body and soul, so that we may lose neither comfort in this world nor fruition of God in the next. We shall get on all right if we hold fast to virtue, but it will mean going at the pace of a hen, and will never lead us to spiritual freedom. This is a procedure which seems to me quite good for people who are in the married state and have to live in accordance with their vocation.

ST TERESA OF AVILA
E. Allison Peers, The Life of Saint Teresa of Avila

Old couples
Contrary to what we are told, and are shouted at on every conceivable level, the couple is one of the great successes of man. It is said that happy couples have no history. That is rubbish. You only have to see in the street an old couple walking hand in hand, supporting each other. They tell of the oldest and most beautiful story in our civilization. One must never put the relationship of a man and a woman solely on the level of sex.

ROMAIN GARY
Paris Match, 1972

Honesty and the family

The thing of demanding honesty of people is in the upper
reaches of extreme innocence. The only people of whom you
can demand honesty are those you pay to get it from. When
you ask [someone] to be honest with you, you are asking him
to act like God, whom he is not, but whom he makes some
attempt to be like by giving you what you want, and it doesn't
make him show up too well, of course. Never, above all things,
ask your family to be honest with you. This is putting a strain
on the human frame it can't bear. [A person's] honesty is only
honesty, not truth, and it can't be of much value to you
intellectually or otherwise. To love people you have to ignore a
good deal of what they say while they are being honest,
because you are not living in the Garden of Eden any longer.

FLANNERY O'CONNOR
The letters of Flannery O'Connor, edited by Sally Fitzgerald

Holy Orders

Many priests are no longer quite sure of the purpose for which
they were ordained. Most of them were trained in fully Christian
conditions. So you can imagine the confusion and suffering that
many priests are now experiencing. Laymen should try to
sympathize with their priests. At the moment, the laity seems
to have a more balanced view of things than the clergy does;
yet the Church is in great need of priests. You might even say
that it is up to the laity to retrain their priests, by showing
them what they expect of them. In the interim, the crisis will
inevitably be accompanied by a slowing down or even a halt in
priestly vocations.

Priests, now being in doubt about the practical nature of their mission, have an added difficulty in being uncertain about their status in society. No one can live without belonging to some community or other. The modern world insists, more than ever, that a man should have a station in life: and this is normally afforded by the sort of work which he does – a professor has his standing in relation to his colleagues and his pupils. Similarly a workman or an engineer has his standing in society determined by the sort of work he does … And the sort of work he does usually provides an environment as well. … And what about the priest? In a Christian environment and in a Christian community, he has his position as a priest. But in other circumstances, his position becomes a hard one. It can become painful and too onerous to bear. A Christian community supports the priest because his priestly activities are necessary to that community; and the community benefits from them, recognizes their importance and wants the priest to provide them. But in a secularized, atheistic society what is the priest to do? … Rather than be condemned to live in almost intolerable loneliness and frustration, he feels impelled to seek some human community to which he feel he can belong. This will probably be the company of his brother-priests … . Well and good. But even while falling back on clerical society he worries about having cut himself off from the people to whom he has been sent by virtue of his priesthood. And if he wants to find a place in ordinary society, he may be tempted to do this by getting married and taking a job. We can only emphasize that the priest must be carried, understood, loved and supported by the Christian community.

RENÉ VOILLAUME
Faith and Contemplation

CONTEMPLATION

The contemplative is not the man who has fiery visions ...
but simply he who has risked his mind in the desert beyond
language and beyond ideas, where God is encountered in the
nakedness of pure trust; that is to say, in the nakedness of our
own poverty and incompleteness, in order no longer to clench
our minds in a cramp as if thinking made us exist.

THOMAS MERTON
Monastic Apology

It has been said that the safety of a nation depends upon the
number of its contemplatives ... while they contemplate the
supernal worlds, they become filled with heavenly peace, after
which Divine light and love flow through them to the earth.

There is a pool of tranquillity within each one of us, a centre
of silence and peace. There the whole being may be renewed.
There the strength of the Father may be felt. To sit beside this
pool once a day at least is to replenish and rejuvenate our being.

Without this period of silence and contemplation our whole
life starts to disintegrate. We have cut ourselves off from our
source and from our purpose.

HENRY THOMAS HAMBLIN
My Search for the Truth

Men immersed in worldly affairs should not say that solitaries are inactive or idle. If by idle they mean that hermits neither buy nor sell, nor build, nor navigate, nor engage in law suits, nor raise children, then such a condemnation would likewise apply to the holy angels of God.

PAUL GIUSTINIANI

Quoted by Robin Bruce-Lockhart in Halfway to Heaven

A day in the life of a Carthusian

No organ or other musical instrument accompanies the Carthusian chant, and in his liturgy the Carthusian seems to be projected by its sacred power to a point where eternity meets his temporal existence.

The Carthusian day begins at 11.45 pm. The monk rises to say the Little Office of our Lady.

The great night vigil of Matins and Lauds ... lasts some two or three hours, and normally in the course of the week all 150 psalms will be sung.

The night vigil over, some time between 2.30 and 3 am, the father returns to his cell to sleep until 6.45, when he rises once more to say the Little Office of Our Lady. This is followed, again in cell, by the ancient office of Prime, which consists of three psalms, the creed, a hymn and some readings. The two offices together will occupy him for some twenty-five minutes.

Prime over, from about 7.15 am the Carthusian father spends the next three-quarters of an hour in private prayer. At 8 am the Little Office of Our Lady is said again, followed by the office of Terce which, with its three psalms, is very similar to Prime.

At 8.15 am the monk leaves his cell for the second time to attend a communal Mass in the monastery church. (The taking of communion is optional at the Mass, since all the fathers say their own individual Masses in small private chapels in the course of the day, at a time usually of their own choosing.)

The Carthusian Mass has been little changed in the course of a thousand years. Shorter than the Tridentine and modern rites, it is of beautiful simplicity. As an act of humility and thanksgiving, the Carthusian will spend a time prostrate on the ground during Mass, be it a conventual or an individual Mass. (Most, though not all, Charterhouses have a chapel attached, with access from outside the monastery, where on Sunday one of the Carthusian fathers will celebrate Mass for the general public.)

Following Mass, and until 11.15 am, the Carthusian devotes himself in his cell to spiritual exercises, prayer, reading and absorbing the Scriptures in *lectio divina*. No special methods of prayer are laid down: each monk is free to follow the path from which he hopes to reap the most fruit. At 11.15 am, still in cell, the Little Office of Our Lady is again recited before the Office of Sext, which is very similar to that of Prime and Terce.

Then, at 11.30 am, having had nothing to eat since 5 pm the day before, the Carthusian father has dinner, brought to him in a 'gamelle' – a kind of billycan – by a brother and passed to him through a hatch in the wall of his cell. Reading, perhaps one of the lives of the Desert Fathers, he will eat slowly, finishing at about 12.30pm. Until 1.15pm, his time is his own in which to relax or do some work in his cell: cleaning it, perhaps doing some washing, or mending.

At 1.15pm the church bell peals, as it has for the other offices, to announce Nones. Similar to the office of Prime, Terce and Sex, it too is said alone in cell, again preceded by the Little Office of Our Lady.

For the next two hours, until 3.30pm, the father remains in his cell, praying privately and perhaps attending to his small garden or undertaking some woodwork before Vespers at 3.45 pm, when he goes to meet his brethren in church for the third and last time of his day, and when the Little Office of our Lady is recited yet again.

When the great church bell peals out the call for Vespers, as each monk enters the church he takes a brief pull on the bell rope before proceeding to his place in the choir stalls. Vespers, which includes four psalms, a hymn, and the Salve Regina, lasts for half an hour.

On returning to his cell after Vespers, the Carthusian Father spends half an hour in prayer, reading and studying before his supper, which is brought to him by a brother at 4.45pm. After supper he will spend about another two and a half hours in spiritual exercises.

The last angelus of the day is tolled at 6.45pm. Some time between then and 7.30 pm the Carthusian, still in his cell, says Compline, followed by the Little Office of Our Lady, which includes three psalms.

And so to bed at 8pm. It has been an intensely busy day: busy with intense prayer and busy with tranquil activity. Time seems to be at a premium in a Charterhouse; the only complaint of the monks seems to be that there are insufficient hours in the day to fit in all the prayer they would like. In fact, after eliminating time spent sleeping, eating, tending to his cell and doing a little manual work, the Carthusian spends some fourteen hours a day in prayer, lectio divina and study, six of these hours in church and eight alone in his cell.

ROBIN BRUCE-LOCKHART
Halfway to Heaven

In a still small voice

Not in the midst of life's tumult, nor in the world of pleasures round, does God show himself, but in the inspiration of nature, grace, light as a breath of fresh air, in a still small voice.

ST JEROME
Commentary on St Matthew's Gospel

THE BEAUTY OF THE WORLD

Sometimes, perhaps, on a clear night, you will have gazed up at the inexpressible beauty of the stars and thought of the author of the universe. You will have wondered who it is who sowed flowers so prettily in the sky where here below necessity takes precedence over charm. Perhaps during the day too you have given thought to the endless array of wonders under the sun, and have risen from visible things to divine the invisible.

ST BASIL
Nine Homilies

Thus I went wide-where, walking alone,
In a wide wilderness, by a woodside,
Bliss of the birds song made me abide there,
And on a lawn, under a linden I leaned a while
To listen to their lays, their lovely notes;
The mirth of their mouths made me to sleep
And midst that bliss dreamed marvellously.
William Langland

WILLAM LANGLAND
Piers Plowman

The love we feel for the splendour of the heavens, the plains, the sea and the mountains, for the silence of nature which is borne in upon us by its thousands of tiny sounds, for the breath of the winds, or the warmth of the sun, this love of which every human being has at least an inkling, is an incomplete, painful love, because it is felt for things which are incapable of responding, that is to say for matter.

SIMONE WEIL
Waiting on God

The beauty of the world has two edges, one of laughter, one of anguish, cutting the heart asunder.

VIRGINIA WOOLF

On Sundays, the noises of village life stop, but at mid morning the church bells start pealing and a grave procession moves slowly down the main unpaved village road. The peasants all wear shoes on these occasions, and are dressed in their festive Sunday clothes – the women have elaborately embroidered camisoles over their white blouses, and the men's heads are covered by black hats with stiff broad brims pierced by an aslant feather. They all walk together in a slow, common rhythm singing sweet naive melodies about Jesus and Mary. And at night, as I fall asleep, I sometimes hear the peasants coming back from the fields and meadows, singing fierce, pure, modal songs that sound like no other music I've heard – and then I am filled by *tesknota,** though I don't know for what.

EVA HOFFMAN
Lost in Translation

tesknota is a Polish word meaning sadness and longing.

Long have I known the glory of it all,
But never knew I this:
Here such a passion is
        As stretches one apart, Lord I do fear
        Thou madest the world too beautiful this year;
My soul is all but out of me, let fall no
Burning leaf; prithee let no bird call.

EDNA ST VINCENT MILLAY
God's World

Hymn to matter

Blessed be you, harsh matter, barren rock; you who yield only
to violence, you who force us to work if we would eat. Blessed
be you, perilous matter, violent sea, untameable passion: you
who, unless we fetter you, will devour us. Blessed be you,
mighty matter, irresistible march of evolution, reality ever
new-born; you who, by constantly shattering our mental
categories, force us to go ever further in our pursuit of the
truth. Blessed be you, universal matter, immeasurable time,
boundless ether, triple abyss of stars and atoms and generations;
you who by overflowing and dissolving our narrow standards
of measurement reveal to us the dimensions of God.

TEILHARD DE CHARDIN
Trans. Bernard Wall

The earth is not an encumbrance, nor an unfortunate accident,
it is a God-given palace.

OSIP MANDELSTAM
Nadezhda Mandelstam, Hope against Hope

In ancient times the love of the beauty of the world had a very
important place in men's thoughts and surrounded the whole
of life with marvellous poetry. This was the case in every nation;
in China, in India, and in Greece ... a sense of beauty, although
mutilated, distorted and soiled, remains rooted in the heart of
man as a powerful incentive. The sense of beauty is present in
all the preoccupations of secular life. If it were made true and
pure it would sweep all secular life to the feet of God.

SIMONE WEIL
Waiting for God

**My happy eyes, everything that you have seen,
whatever it may be, was yet so beautiful.**

JOHANN WOLFGANG VON GOETHE

Tempo era dal principio del mattino;
E il sol montava in su con quelle stelle
Ch'eran con lui, quando l'amor divino
Mossi di prima quelle cose belle.

It was daybreak and the sun arose,
Together with him some stars,
When the Divine Love
First moved its beautiful works

DANTE

Inferno, 1st canto, trans. Lawrence Binyon

The gate of beauty

Into the great temple of truth, there are two gates – the gate of Wisdom and the gate of beauty. I am inclined to think that the gate of wisdom is the narrow gate, and the wide gate through which millions pass is the gate of beauty. I believe the way of beauty is the wiser as well as the wider way. It is God's own most perfect way to Himself.

VINCENT MCNABB

Bliss

Now may every living thing, feeble or strong, omitting none, or tall or middlesized or short, subtle or gross, seen or unseen, those dwelling near or far away – whether they be born or yet unborn —— may every living thing be full of bliss.

SAYINGS OF THE BUDDHA
Trans. F. L. Woodward

228

MYSTERY

Mystery – Doctrine of faith involving difficulties which human reason is incapable of solvng. A hidden or secret thing beyond human knowledge or comprehension.

OXFORD ENGLISH DICTIONARY

The incomprehensibility of God is the definitive blessing, the alpha and the omega of reality, behind which there is nothing and before which there can be nothing.

The mystery is the one thing that is self-explanatory, the one thing that is its own sufficient reason. It has always been familiar to us and we have always loved it.

KARL RAHNER
The Concept or Mystery in Catholic Theology

The most beautiful and the most profound emotion we can experience is the sensation of the mystical. It is the source of all true science. He to whom this emotion is a stranger, who can no longer wonder and stand rapt in awe, is as good as dead.

To know that what is impenetrable to us really exists, manifesting itself as the highest wisdom and the most radiant beauty which our dull faculties can comprehend only in their most primitive forms – this knowledge, this feeling is at the centre of our religiousness.

ALBERT EINSTEIN
The World and Doctor Einstein

Ogni cosa è fatto con misterio e per amore.
All things are done with mystery and because of love.

ST CATHERINE OF SIENA

There's not the smallest orb which thou behold'st,
But in his motion like an angel sings,
Such harmony is in immortal souls;
But while this muddy vesture of decay
Doth grossly close it in, we cannot hear it.

WILLIAM SHAKESPEARE

The Merchant of Venice

The great secret, the great mystery: there is a heart in the
world and this heart is the heart of Christ.

TEILHARD DE CHARDIN

Robert Speaight, Teilhard de Chardin: A Biography

In the dreaming
There seems to have been a continual preoccupation with the
mystery of life and death, and all that was unknown or not
physically present at a given moment was referred to as 'in
the dreaming'.

BRUCE CHATWIN

The Australian Aborigine

230

There was no wind, the air was cold and and there was a great silence, except for a faint sighing in the trees, as if they were breathing easily in their sleep, not yet ready to wake. For a moment the world seemed at peace and if ever I felt the presence of God walking in it, this was the moment.
If only it could have lasted for ever.

ERIC NEWBY
Love and War in the Appenines

A point of nothingness

At the centre of our being is a point of nothingness which is untouched by sin and illusion, a point of pure truth, a point or spark which belongs entirely to God, which is never at our disposal, from which God disposes of our lives, which is inaccessible to the fantasies of our own mind or the brutalities of our own will. This little point of nothingness and of absolute poverty is the pure glory of God in us. It is, so to speak, His name written in us as our poverty, our indigence, as our dependence, our sonship. It is like a pure diamond, blazing with the light of heaven. It is in everybody, and if we could see it, we would see these billions of points of light coming together in the blaze of the sun that would make the darkness and cruelty of life vanish completely. The gate of heaven is everywhere.

THOMAS MERTON
The Sign of Jonas

There is nothing in the world that is not God…it is undying, blazing spirit wherein lies hidden the world and its creatures.

UPANISHADS

Now where the wheeling systems darken,
And our benumbed conceiving soars,
The drift of pinions, would we hearken,
Beats at our own clayshutter'd doors.

The angels keep their ancient places,
Turn but a stone and start a wing! 'Tis ye,
'Tis your estrangéd faces,
That miss the many splendour'd thing.

But (when so sad thou canst not sadder)
Cry!; and upon thy most sore loss
Shall shine the traffic of Jacob's ladder,
Pitched between heaven and Charing Cross.

Yea, in the night, my Soul, my daughter
Cry!; clinging heaven by the hems;
And low, Christ walking on the waters,
Not of Genasareth but the Thames.

FRANCIS THOMPSON
The Kingdom of God

E'n la sua voluntade è nostra pace
His will, our peace.

DANTE
Paradiso III, 85

Then did I dwell, within a world of light,
Distinct and separate from all men's sight,
Where I did feel strange thoughts and saw such things
That were, or seemed, only revealed to me,
No ear but eyes were all the hearers there,
And every stone and every star a tongue,
And every gale of wind a curious song.

THOMAS TRAHERNE
Dumbness

With equal passion I have sought knowledge. I have wished to
understand the hearts of men. I have wished to know why the
stars shine. And I have tried to apprehend the Pythagorian
theory by which number holds sway above the flux.

BERTRAND RUSSELL
from the Preface to his Autobiography

Le silence éternel de ces espaces infinies m'effraie.
The eternal silence of infinite space frightens me.

BLAISE PASCAL
Pensées

Eternal life

We said then: 'if the tumult of the flesh were hushed; hushed
these shadows of earth, sea and sky; hushed the heavens and
the soul itself, so that it should pass beyond itself, and not think
of itself; if all dreams were hushed and all sensuous revelations,
and every tongue and every symbol; if all that comes and goes
were hushed. They all proclaim to him that hath an ear: "We
made not ourselves: He made us who abideth forever" – But
suppose that, having delivered their message, they held their
peace, turning their ear to Him who made them and that He
alone spoke, not by any fleshly tongue, nor by any angel's voice,
but His voice whom we love in these His creatures – Suppose
we heard Him without any intermediary at all – Just now we
reached out, and with one flash of thought, touched the Eternal
Wisdom that abides above all – Suppose this endured, and all
other visions, so far inferior, were taken away, and this alone
were to ravish the beholder, and absorb him, and plunge him
in mystic joy. Might not eternal life be like this moment of
comprehension for which we sighed?'

ST AUGUSTINE
The Confessions, Book 9

A place in another country

Since we stay not here, being people of a day's abode, and our
age is like that of the flie, and contemporary with a gourd, we
must look somewhere else for an abiding city, a place in another
country to fix our house in.

BISHOP JEREMY TAYLOR
Holy Dying, iii 2

AFTERWORD

The Sacramental Word

I want to look at the event of the Last Supper. The words of
Jesus on that night, 'This is my body, given for you', show the
ultimate vocation of all human speaking. They are words that
transform, that make new. These words transformed betrayal
into the new covenant, death into life. Our preaching is a
breaking of the bread of the word.

I will look at three moments in the event of the Last Supper.

First of all there is the incomprehension of the disciples. They
do not know what is going on. They are silenced.

Secondly, Jesus gathers them into communion in the sharing
of the bread.

Thirdly, he shares the cup that looks forward to the coming
of the Kingdom.

'And as they were sitting at table eating, Jesus said, "Truly I
say to you, one of you will betray me, one who is eating with
me" They began to be sorrowful, and to say to him one after
another, "Is it I?" He said to them, "It is one of the twelve, one
who is dipping bread into the dish with me. For the Son of man
goes as it is written of him, but woe to that man by whom the
Son of man is betrayed." ' Mark 14.17–20

Leonardo Da Vinci's 'Last Supper', in our refectory in Santa
Maria delle Grazie in Milan, shows this moment. It is a moment
of confusion, of puzzlement, of bewilderment. Our eyes are

drawn to Judas, the hidden centre of the drama. As Charles Nicholl says, 'He recoils from the words of Christ even as his hand moves irrevocably towards the piece of bread will dip in the dish.' [1]

We may imagine the disciples coming up to Jerusalem still with hopes for the future. Presumably they imagined the expulsion of the Romans, the anointing of Jesus as King, the coming of the Kingdom. As the disciples say on the way to Emmaus, 'We had hoped that he was the one to redeem Israel.' (Luke 24.21.) But now they lose any story to tell of the future. They are bewildered. This incomprehension is the necessary preparation for the gift that they could never have anticipated, the gift of Jesus' body, the new covenant. They must be silenced before they can hear.

The beginning of our meditation is in embracing that incomprehension, sharing humanity's silence in the face of the gospel. Barbara Brown Taylor wrote, 'In each of the Gospels, the Word comes forth from silence. For John, it is the silence at the beginning of creation. For Luke, it is the silence of poor old Zechariah, struck dumb by the angel Gabriel for doubting that Elizabeth would bear a child. For Matthew, it is the awkward silence between Joseph and Mary when she tells him her prenuptial news. And for Mark, it is the voice of one crying in the wilderness – the long-forgotten voice of prophecy puncturing the silence of the desert and of time.' [2]

One is lost for words. Often this happens because one is struck by some dissonance in the text, something that does not seem right. William Carlos Williams wrote:

1 *Leonardo da Vinci: The Flights of the Mind,* London, 2004
2 *When God is Silent*, Boston, 1998, p.73

'Dissonance
(if you are interested)
leads to discovery.' [3]

Last Sunday, for example, we had the parable of the mustard seed. The first step in preparing oneself to preach is to be puzzled by the text. What is going on here? Why does this mustard seed become a tree. Mustard seeds do not become trees. Something strange is happening. I do not understand. We have nothing to say until we have arrived at the moment of having nothing to say. Then we have to ask the Lord for illumination. It is no coincidence that Dominic wished friars of the Order of Preachers to be beggars. We have to beg for a word.

Simone Weil wrote that 'we do not obtain the most precious gifts by going in search of them but by waiting for them ... This way of looking is, in the first place, attentive.' [4] This waiting is not entirely passive and vacant. One reads commentaries, goes over the text time and time again. One prays. We ask our brethren. Herbert McCabe, the greatest preacher I have ever heard, would sometimes grab the brethren as they passed his room and ask them what I thought the Sunday readings were about, almost in desperation.

We have to give God the time to offer us his word. If it is a gift, then we cannot determine when it will be given. We cannot tell God that it is his duty to produce the goods between 9 and 10pm on the Saturday night, which is the time that we

3 Paterson IV, quoted Hugh Payment-Pickard *Myths of Time: from St Augustine to American Beauty*, London, 2004, p. 1

4 *Waiting for God*, London, 1959, p.169

have put aside to prepare the sermon. He gives when he wishes, and we must be around to receive the gift then. Wittgenstein was asked how philosophers should greet each other, and he replied that they should say to each other, 'Take your time'. As friars preachers, that is what we need to say to each other too. Give God time, so that he may give us the word.

Annie Dillard captures well the combination of gift and hard grind that is involved: 'At its best, the sensation of writing is that of any unmerited grace. It is handed to you, but only if you look for it. You search, you break your heart, your back, your brain and then – and only then – it is handed to you. From the corner of your eye you can see motion. Something is moving the air and headed your way.' [5]

Now, after this incomprehension, the disciples are ready to receive the unexpected gift of Jesus' words. Mark writes. 'And as they were eating, he took bread, and blessed, and broke it, and gave it to them, and said, "Take; this is my body."' (Mark 14.22)

Jesus presides at the Last Supper. He is the host. He offers them the hospitality of the Passover feast, and ultimately the hospitality of the new covenant, his own body. The words that we offer should be hospitable. The preacher is inviting people to find their home in God's word, somewhere they may belong.

One of the earliest great preaching missions of the Order in collaboration with the Franciscans was 'The Great Devotion' of 1233. [6] Most of the cities of northern Italy were suffering from clashes between factions and were virtually in civil war.

5 ibid., p.75

6 c.f. Augustine Thompson OP, *Revival Preachers and Politics in Thirteenth-Century Italy: The Great Devotion of 1233*, Oxford, 1992

The preaching was not just summoning people to live in peace. It was itself a peace-making. Often the climax of the sermon was a ritual kiss of peace exchanged between enemies. As preachers the friars were often authorized to ordain the release of prisoners, the forgiveness of debts, and even to rewrite the civil statutes. No one has ever asked me to do that, thanks be to God.

Shortly before he died Cornelius Ernst wrote in his diary, 'I cannot allow that God can only be adored in spirit and in truth by the individual introverted upon himself and detached from all that might disturb and solicit his heart. It must be possible to find and adore God in the complexity of human experience.'

This belongs to the very meaning of the offering of the bread and wine that we share. Geoffrey Preston, one of my many student masters, wrote: 'Think of domination, exploitation and pollution of man and nature that goes with bread, all the bitterness of competition and class struggle, all the organized selfishness of tariffs and price-rings, all the wicked oddity of a world distribution that brings plenty to some and malnutrition to others, bringing them to that symbol of poverty we call the bread line. And wine too – fruit of the vine and work of human hands, the wine of holidays and weddings … This wine is also the bottle, the source of some of the most tragic forms of human degradation: drunkenness, broken homes, sensuality, debt. What Christ bodies himself into is bread and wine like this, and he manages to make sense of it, to humanize it. Nothing human is alien to him. If we bring bread and wine to the Lord's table, we are implicating ourselves in being prepared to bring to God all that bread and wine mean. We are implicating ourselves in bringing to God, for him to make sense of, all which is broken and unlovely. We are implicating ourselves in the sorrow as well as the joy of the world.'[7] Our words should offer a space for all the pain and the joy that people bring with them as they gather around the altar.

St Thomas loved the gospel text which says that we should call no one master, for we have one who is in heaven. I noticed that the brethren also seemed to like this text when I was Master of the Order, for it appeared to crop up in the readings with suspicious frequency! Thomas understood that it is God who teaches through grace in the depths of the human heart and mind. All that a human teacher can do is to accompany people in their exploration, sharing in friendship what we have received. Josef Pieper expresses Thomas' view in this way: 'A friend, and a prudent friend, can help to share a friend's decision. He does so by virtue of that love which makes the friend's problem his own, the friend's ego his own (so that it is not entirely "from outside").'[8] We have to become that other person, enter their imagination and share their dilemmas, as we share our teaching.

This sympathy does not imply that one must not challenge people, refuse easy compromises, and confront them with the demands of the gospel. The sermon of Antonio de Montesinos in 1511 is an obvious example for us Dominicans, confronting the Spaniards with their cruelty to the indigenous people of Hispaniola. But the greatest challenge, it seems to me, is for the preacher to find a way through to a language that is capacious enough, which carries people beyond the ideological discourses

7 *God's Way to be Man*, London, 1978, p. 84
8 *The Four Cardinal Virtues*, Notre Dame, 1966, p.29

of left and right, and which offers people something of the spaciousness of God's word.

It is hard to imagine a greater betrayal of the Dominican vocation than to succumb to the temptation of preaching ideology, using the pulpit to push a party line. In the seventeenth century, when Jesuits and Dominican were locked in terrible battles about grace, the pulpit was called, 'the lectureship in revenge.'[9] Every sermon was an opportunity to attack the opposition. But this is in contradiction with the very nature of preaching the gospel.

Of course each of us is the fruit of our own history. We talk with particular accents, American and British, liberal or conservative. We have our sympathies and antipathies. Our imaginations are ignited by particular traditions. There is no universal ecclesiastical Esperanto, some ideal way of talking that is beyond all division, neutral and pure. Yet despite that every preacher is challenged to open up his imagination and sympathy to those who think differently, who belong to other camps and allegiances in the Church. We have to develop what Thomas Aquinas calls *latitudo cordis*, the stretching open of our hearts. This is much more than mere tolerance of people who are different. It is the creative task of finding new words, or rediscovering old words, which open up spaces in which people who disagree may find themselves at home. It is learning Christ's hospitality.

In *Larry's Party* the Canadian novelist Carol Shields explores how language offers us a home to live in. Larry's first marriage broke up because he and his young wife did not have a

9 '*A question of Rites: Friar Domingo Navarrete and the Jesuits in China*', Aldershot, 1993, p.46

language that was large enough for them to find and love each other. Finally when they are reconciled it is because their language is spacious enough for them to be together for the first time. Larry asks, 'Was that our problem? That we didn't know enough words?' [10] One challenge for preaching in the West today is learning enough words, other people's words, so that God's wide open home can be spoken. Every proclamation of the faith should extend the vocabulary a little, stretch the heart a bit wider.

Towards the end of *A Midsummer Night's Dream*, Theseus says,

> The forms of things unknown the poet's pen
> Turns them into shapes, and gives to airy nothing
> A local habitation and a name. (V.i)

That is the preacher's task, to create a local habitation and a name, to open up a passage into the unexpected spaciousness of the new covenant.

If we try to be attentive to other ways of understanding the gospel, and open our minds to other ways of speaking, then we shall risk being taken to task by those to whom we are close. We may be suspected of becoming unsound, of losing our doctrinal purity, of not standing by the party line. That is the risk that we preachers must take if we are to offer an hospitable word.

10 London, 1998, p. 336

Sharing the cup

> And he took a cup, and when he had given thanks he gave
> it to them, and they all drank of it. And he said to them,
> 'This is my blood of the covenant, which is poured out
> for many. Truly, I say to you, I shall not drink again of the
> fruit of the vine until that day when I drink it new in the
> kingdom of God.' (14.23–25)

The slight difference between words about the bread and
the cup are key. The bread is given to the disciples. The cup is
shared with them, but is also poured out for the *many*. It will
not be drunk again by Jesus until the Kingdom. The bread is
to given to that small community, which Jesus has gathered
around him. His disciples share it together. The cup looks
forward to the Kingdom, into which all are called.

This is a tension that is intrinsic to every Eucharist. The
Church lives from its dynamism. The Eucharist is both
centripetal and centrifugal; it gathers in and it sends out.
The very word 'Mass' comes from our final dismissal. This
tension between the bread and the cup at the heart of being
Roman Catholic. For to be Roman is to be gathered into a
particular community. We are heirs of a particular tradition,
or rather web of traditions. We have inherited ways of talking
and thinking, praying and governing, living and dying. We are
bound together as this particular community by communion
with the See of Rome. But we are also Catholic, which means
that we reach out to universality, open to the unimaginable
diversity of human cultures and wisdom. This means that we
are always a little impatient with any identity which seems

closed and finished and defined. We are on the way to the
Kingdom and there will discover the secret of our identity
hidden in Christ. This tension between our identity as both
known and hidden appears in the First letter of St John.
'Beloved, we are God's children *now*; it does not *yet* appear
what we shall be, but we know that when he appears we
shall be like him, for we shall see him as he is.' (3.2f).

The challenge is keep that tension dynamic and alive. If
we become just Roman, then we may become just a sect,
an introverted group of people with a private language, the
Fortress Church, confident of its identity but closed. We
would not be a sign of the Kingdom. But if we become just
Catholic and lose that rootedness in the particularity of our
community, then we will be in danger of becoming just a
vague moment, the Jesus people, shuffling chaotically in no
discernible direction. We would not either be a sign of the
Kingdom. Which means that the Church can only be a sign
of the Kingdom if it is an identifiable 'we', but a 'we' that is
always being torn open in the outreach to 'the all'.

Herbert McCabe OP wrote: 'Our language does not
encompass but simply strains towards the mystery that
we encounter in Christ. … The theologian uses a word by
stretching it to breaking point, and it is precisely as it breaks
that the communication, if any, is achieved.' [11]

Stretching language to breaking point is a poetic task. It is
poetry that renews our language by pushing it beyond what
can be said easily and literally. This is beautifully described by
Seamus Heaney describes a poem by Dylan Thomas as giving

11 *God Matters*, London, 1987, p.177

'the sensation of language on the move towards a destination in knowledge'.[12] We can preach the Kingdom in language that is on the way towards a destination in knowledge, as we stretch our minds and words towards a fullness that cannot be captured. Heaney even describes this poetic function in a way that is highly evocative of the Eucharist itself: 'We go to poetry, we go to literature in general, to be forwarded within ourselves. The best it can do is to give us an experience that is like foreknowledge of certain things which we already seem to be remembering.'[13] This foreknowledge which is also a remembering suggests the dynamic of the Eucharist which is both a remembrance – 'Do this in memory of me' – and also a promise of an unsayable future.

Not every preacher is a poet but we need language that is kept alive, electric, tense and vibrant by poets. And this is one reason for the crisis of preaching today. The poetic imagination is marginal within our dominant scientific culture which tends towards a deadening literalism, what Yann Martel calls a 'dry yeastless factuality.'[14] In most traditional societies, poetry, myth, song and music have been central to the culture. In our society these have often been reduced to mere entertainment and so it is harder for the preacher to evoke that ultimate human destiny which transcends our words. If the preaching of the word of God is to flourish, then we need poets and artists, singers and musicians who keep alive that intuition of our ultimate destiny.

12 ibid., p.141.
13 ibid., p.159.
14 Yann Martel, *The Life of Pi*, p.64.

Conclusion

So I have looked at three moments in Mark's account of the Last Supper: the bewilderment of the disciples faced with the betrayal of Jesus; the gathering into communion with the gift of Christ's body, and the reaching out for the Kingdom with the sharing of the cup.

Some hint of this dynamism of this event should infect us if it is in any way to share with others the happening of grace, 'the genetic moment.' This sounds awfully ambitious and no sermon, and perhaps no brother, can ever achieve all that. We *all* need to begin by becoming beggars for the word, waiting in silence for the word that is to be given. That is common to all preaching. But some of us will be better at gathering people into communion and others at reaching out for the Kingdom alone.

We can see a rhythm here. Jesus reaches out to the silence of the disciples, and gathers them into his community, and then reaches out to the Kingdom. This is like the tempo of breathing, the filling and emptying of lungs. The vital moments of the history of our salvation are always moments of the filling and emptying of humanity's lungs. God breathes into the lungs of Adam at the beginning, then Christ breathes out his last breath on the cross, and then the Holy Spirit is breathed into our lungs again at Pentecost. Finally note that this dramatic event of the Last Supper moves us from the silence of incomprehension to the silence of the mystery, from an empty silence to a plenary silence. We go from the silence of the disciples who understand nothing, to the silence of those who cannot find adequate words for what they have glimpsed. The preacher lives within that space, begging for a word. It is the gift of God's grace, what the early Dominicans called the *gratia praedicationis*, that propels us from that silence of poverty to that silence that is full.

INDEX OF AUTHORS

I have put all contemporary authors on the same brief footing so as not to appear to favour some rather than others. Also I have left out of this index figures who are house-hold names such as Roosevelt, Napoleon, and some others. If the reader notices some gaps it will be for this reason.

known books are *Cautionary Tales for Children* and *The Bad Child's Book of Beasts*.

San Bernardino of Siena, 1380–1444. Franciscan friar, 'the People's Preacher'.

Betjeman, Sir John, 1906–64. One of the most popular and widely read poets of twentieth-century Britain. Also and architectural writer and critic, especially on Victorian England.

Blake, William, 1757–1827. Artist and poet. Contemporaries were suspicious of his real and literary visions. He was considered gifted but insane. However, his attack on eighteenth-century materialism and also on the puritanical narrowness of contemporary Christianity was prophetic.

Blanch, Stuart, 1918–94. Archbishop of York 1975–83.

Bonhoeffer, Dietrich, 1906–45. German Lutheran theologian. Hanged by the Nazis for his part in a conspiracy against Hitler.

Boylan, Eugene, 1904–64. Irish Cistercian, linguist, confessor. His best-known work is *This Tremendous Lover*.

Brennan Gerald, 1919–87. Contemporary English writer, renowned for his books on Spain, where he lived most of his life.

Brown, T(homas) E(dward), 1830–97. He was born in the Isle of Man. His best non-dialect poems showed a great love of the West country

landscape and are a lot better than the often anthologized piece 'A garden is a lovesome thing, God wot'.

Bruce-Lockhart, Robin. Contemporary writer, stockbroker and newspaper executive.

St Bruno, c.1033–1101. Born in Cologne, died in Calabria. Founder of the Carthusian Order. Established the great monastery called the Grande Chartreuse (which still exists).

Bunson, Anna. I have taken this poem from a wonderful book called *English Spirituality*. The authors of this book could not find out much about Anna Bunston except what I put here – that she became Mrs Bunston de Bary and had a book of collected poems published in 1947.

Burrows, Sister Ruth, b.1929. Writer and Carmelite nun.

Calvino, Italo, 1923–85.Born in Cuba, died in Siena. Writer and journalist. He joined the Italian Resistance, worked for the Communist newspaper *l' Unita* and then for the publishers Einaudi. An experimental writer who used shifting viewpoints and innovative structures. He wrote the mock chivalrous epic *The Cloven Viscount*, *Invisible Cities*, and essays on the *Use of Literature*.

Camus, Albert, 1913–60. Born in Mondavi in Algeria, died in a car accident in France. Philosophy graduate. Active in French

Resistance. Playwright and writer of clear-sighted and spare prose that illuminates the human conscience. His best-known novels are *L'Etranger* and *La Peste*, also the essay the *Le Mythe de Sisyphe*. Won the Nobel Prize for Literature in 1957.

Casals, Pablo. Born in Catalonia, died in Puerto Rico. Great cellist and conductor. Ardent Republican. Conductor and cellist in the Prades Festival, he gave master classes all over the world.

Cather, Willa 1873–1947. Born in Blue Ridge Mountains, Virginia. Moved to Nebraska where she went to university. Won the Pulitzer prize for *One of Ours*. Among her other great books were *O Pioneers* and *Death Comes for the Archbishop*.

Catherine of Aragon, 1485–1536. Daughter of Ferdinand and Isabella of Spain. First wife of Henry VIII. Bore Henry six children (three boys who died). Endured his infidelities. Refused to divorce him so that he could marry Anne Boleyn.

St Catherine of Siena, 1347–80. Mediated between Florence and the Papal States. Persuaded Pope Gregory XI to return from Avignon to Rome. Patron Saint of Italy.

Chantal, Suzanne. Contemporary and friend of André Malraux and wrote of his life with Josette Clotis, the mother of his sons.

Chesterton, G(ilbert) K(enneth), 1874–1936. A biographer, mystery writer, literary critic, political analyst, essayist, humorist and poet. Received into the Catholic Church in 1922. *The Everlasting Man*, an outline of Christianity, was declared by C. S. Lewis to be the contemporary book that had most helped him.

Crowley, John. Catholic Bishop of Middlesborough.

Chatwin, Bruce, 1940–81. Novelist and travel writer. He first worked in Sotheby's, before winning the Hawthendon Prize in 1978 for his first book *In Patagonia*. He wrote books as diverse as *On the Black Hill*, about identical twins in mid Wales, and *Songlines*, about the Aborigines in Australia.

Dante, Alighieri, 1265–1321. The great poet of the high Renaissance. He came from the minor Florentine aristocracy and was active in Florentine politics as a *prior* (chief magistrate). As a member of the White Guelphs he was dispossessed and banished from Florence by the Black Guelphs, and spent the rest of his life wandering in northern and central Italy. Not long after he had written the last lines of *The Divine Comedy* (which he took fourteen years to write), he died in Ravenna, where he is buried.

Davies, W. H., 1871–1940. English poet. Lived as a tramp for some years in the USA and then in England. Most of his poetry is short and joyful except for *Nell Bridges* (about prostitution) and *Australian Bill* (about alcoholism).

Dickinson, Emily, 1830–86. America's greatest woman poet born and died in Amherst, Massachusetts. She lived an enclosed puritan life as housekeeper to her father and died aged 56 leaving 1,700 poems, only 2 of which were published in her lifetime – and those without her consent.

Dinesen, Isak, 1885–1962 (Karen Christence Blixen-Fineke). Danish writer and storyteller *par excellence*. Her best known work in English is *Out of Africa*, about the farm she owned in Kenya, which was made into an Oscar-winning film. Another great work is the *Seven Gothic Tales*.

Donne, John, 1572–1631. Dean of St Paul's Cathedral. His sermons are still some of the best in the English language.

Dorotheus, c.255–c.362. Dorotheus was a writer, scholar and priest. He lived to a great age and was martyred for his faith.

Dostoievsky, Fyodor, 1821–81. Born in Moscow, he came from a decaying noble family and struggled for years against poverty and illness. He joined a revolutionary group whose activities condemned Dostoievsky, his brother and thirty others to death. While the group were on their way to the scaffold the sentence was commuted to four years in Siberia. Those years of dreadful suffering sowed the seeds of his greatest work, *Crime and Punishment*.

Dyer, Sir Edward, 1543–1607. A poet and statesman, Lord Chancellor under Elizabeth I, and a Knight of the Garter. He was a friend of Spencer and Philip Sydney.

Eckhart, Maester 1260?–1327. Great German Dominican and mystic.

Einstein, Albert, 1879–1955. Having failed his engineering exams, Einstein left Germany for Switzerland where, in 1905, he wrote the paper which today is called 'The theory of relativity'. In 1921 he won the Nobel Prize. He left Europe when the Nazis came to power, and lived mainly in the United States.

Eliot, George, 1819–88. Pseudonym of Mary Ann Evans, daughter of a Warwickshire farm manager. Her great novels, first *Adam Bede* then *The Mill on the Floss* and *Silas Marner*, were admired by Charles Dickens and Wilkie Collins.

Elizabeth I, 1533–1603. She inherited a land bled dry by Mary Tudor, but her 44-year reign became one of the high points of English history. In Elizabethan England, Shakespeare, Marlowe and Spencer were at work, while Raleigh and Drake extended English power into the New World.

Fitzgerald, Penelope. Contemporary English writer.

St Francis de Sales, 1567–1622. Born near Annecy, died at Lyons. Doctor of the Church and Bishop of Geneva. Founder together with St Jeanne de Chantal of the Visitation nuns. Friend of Henri IV who begged him to help those souls who had to live in the world. His *Introduction to the Devout Life* and the *Treatise on the Love of God*, together with his great sermons taught that 'ordinary' life in the world can be made holy. Patron saint of journalists

St Francis of Assisi, c.1181–1226. Vowed 'to marry Lady Poverty' and founded the Friar Minors, and later with St Clare, the first community of Poor Ladies. He was never a priest but a man of outstanding spiritual insight and power. Often shown in art with the stigmata.

Freud, Sigmund 1856–1939. The founder of psychoanalysis. Born in Moravia, he trained in Vienna. He believed that the goal of therapy was to make the unconscious conscious. He also held that the unconscious sexual drives of infancy and early childhood helped to form the personality. Particularly in the USA, he has had a far reaching influence not only on psychiatry but on social science and society in general. Forced to flee from Nazi Austria in 1938, Freud spent his last years in London.

Furlong, Monica, contemporary English writer and biographer.

Gary, Romain, 1914–80. Born in Vilnius or Moscow. Russian father, French mother. Pilot in Free French forces. Consul in Los Angeles. *Les Racines du Ciel*. Also wrote as Emile Ajar, and won the Prix Goncourt for *La Vie devant Soi*. After death of Jean Seberg in 1979, killed himself in 1980.

Ginsberg, Evgenia. Russian teacher, Communist Party member, arrested and sentenced to life imprisonment. Wrote the classic two-volume work *Into the Whirlwind* and *Within the Whirlwind*.

Giustiniani, Blessed Paul, 1476–1528. He was a Venetian humanist who became a Camaldolese hermit, reformed that very strict Benedictine Order, and wrote many contemplative works.

van Gogh, Vincent, 1853–90. This great Dutch artist died in the asylum (which still exists) in St Rémy de Provence. During his short life he painted a phenomenal number of brilliant neo-Impressionist pictures which, though they now fetch record sums, scarcely paid at the time for his board and lodging.

Goethe, Johann Wolfgang 1749–1832. German poet and playwright. His patron was the Duke of Weimar, whom he followed to France after the invasion of 1792, becoming his councillor and finally Minister of State. A friend of Schiller, he is Germany's foremost poet. His best known work is *Faust*.

General Gordon of Khartoum, 1833–85. Initially known as 'Chinese Gordon'

for putting down the Taiping
Rebellion. Became a national hero
for the second time after his ill-fated
defence of Khartoum from the rebel
leader the Mahdivasin, in which
he died.

St Gregory the Great, c.540–604. Born
and died in Rome. Pope and Doctor
of the Church, first and greatest pope
of that name. Sent first missionaries
to England. First to call himself 'the
servant of the servants of God'.

Guigo II, 1140–93. Ninth Prior of the
Grande Chartreuse. He wrote a
Study of Contemplation known as
The Ladder of Monks from the Bible
story of Jacob's ladder.

Dom Gustavo Gutierrez, born 1928.
Peruvian Catholic theologian.
Considered to be the father of
Liberation Theology.

Hamblin, Henry Thomas, 1873–1968.
Founded magazine *The Science of
Thought*. Most popular books are *My
Search for the Truth* and *The Power of
Thought*.

Harris, Martyn. Contemporary writer
and journalist.

St Helena, c.225–c.330.

Hemming, John. Contemporary English
writer and explorer. Former President
of the Royal Geographical Society.

Herbert, George, 1593–1633. Parish
priest and one of England's foremost
Christian poets.

Herrick, Robert, 1591–1674. Priest
and poet. Lost his living in the Civil

War and for many years lived a
cheerful exile in London.

Hoffman, Eva. Writer, born in Poland
but emigrated to the USA.

Homer, 800 BC. Affluent Greek citizens
liked to hire a professional storyteller as an evening's entertainment
and it is thought that Homer, who
may also have been blind, was one of
these. *The Odyssey* and the *Iliad* are
the most important texts in Greek
culture.

Hopkins, Gerald Manley, 1844–89.
Jesuit priest and great English poet
whose depression and sense of his
poetry being at odds with his vocation
stopped him writing for seven years.

von Hugel, Friedrich, 1852–1925. Son
of an Austrian diplomat who came to
England in his youth and was a devout
Catholic and spiritual director. His
letters to his niece, offering practical
spirituality, became famous.

Hume, Basil, 1923–99. Benedictine
monk, Abbot of Ampleforth and
Cardinal Archbishop of Westminster

Huvelin, Abbé, 1830–1910. Known as
the 'Apostle of Paris'. Famous spiritual
director who reconciled Charles de
Foucauld with the Church.

St Jerome, 331–420. Doctor of the
Latin Church, together with
Augustine, Gregory the Great and
Ambrose of Milan. Born in Dalmatia,
died in Jeruslaem. A vigorous
apologist, he wrote the first
translation of the Bible.

253

St John of the Cross, 1442–1591. Born in Avila, theologian and poet, Doctor of the Church. Carmelite monk of the Reformed order (discalced), founded by Teresa of Avila, whose rigorous spiritual director he also was. His three great poems *The Dark Night*, *The Spiritual Canticle* and *Flame of Living Love* are among the most beautiful in the Spanish language.

Jones, Ernest. American doctor of psychiatry and devoted follower of Freud.

Julian of Norwich, *c.*1342–post 1416. Lived in a cell attached to St Julian's Church in Norwich, hence her name. She had sixteen visions which came to her after an almost fatal illness. She interpreted these 'shewings' over the rest of her life, speaking always of a compassionate and intimate God.

Jung, Carl Gustav, 1875–1961. The great Swiss psychiatrist. He was the son of a pastor. His first meeting with Freud, led Freud to believe he had found his heir apparent. The break between them came because Jung did not agree with Freud's emphasis on sexual trauma. Instead he formed the concept of extroversion and introversion, and also the individual and collective unconscious often revealed in dreams. For a greater part of his life he believed that without a spiritual philosophy man was doomed to unhappiness.

Keble, John, 1792–1866. Born into a High Anglican family. After a successful academic career he became a country parson near Winchester. With Newman he inspired the Anglo-Catholic movement in the Church of England.

Kierkegaard, Søren, 1813–55. Danish philosopher. Born and died in Copenhagen. Profound influence on most twentieth-century philosophers, including such diverse people as Barth, Sartre and Wittgenstein. At heart an evangelist, his whole literary production was an exercise in communicating the Christian message.

Knox, Monsignor Ronald, 1888–1957. Son of the Anglican Bishop of Manchester. His most famous work, *Caliban in Grub Street*, mocks the glib atheism of the English upper classes. A great preacher, he wrote *The Belief of Catholics*.

Langland, William, 1330–86. Little is known about the author of 'Piers Plowman', but much of the poem was an attack on the abuses in the fourteenth-century Church and society.

Law, William, 1686–1761. Law attacked the hypocrites of his time in a book *A Serious Call to the Devout Life*, which gave him a big following. John Wesley was one of his admirers.

Lawrence, Brother (Nicholas Herman) *c.*1605–91. Converted as a soldier of eighteen and became famous for his conversations and letters which, were made into *The Practice of the Presence of God*.

Lawrence, D. H. B. 1885–1930. A miner's son from Nottinghamshire. His early life was spent as a teacher but in he 1909 submitted some poems to the *English Review*, through which he met W. B. Yeats, H. G. Wells and Ezra Pound. He eloped with Frieda von Richtofen, and married her in Metz. He felt strongly that England was finished as a country and died, after living in Mexico, in the South of France. *Lady Chatterly's Lover* was not published in England in its unexpurgated version until 1961.

Lewis, C. S. 1898–1963. The most popular religious writer of the twentieth century. Became a Christian while at Cambridge, where he later taught. Besides his religious works wrote science fiction and the classic Narnia books for children.

Lewis, Norman. Contemporary English traveller and writer.

Lunn, Sir Arnold, 1888–1974. Born in Madras. Father was a medical missionary. Arnold's great love was Switzerland, where he became the father of modern skiing and instituted the slalom and downhill racing. A Catholic convert, he became a controversial writer and Catholic Apologist.

Luther, Martin, 1483–1546. A doctor of philosophy and an Augustine monk. After a voyage to Rome he became a vehement critic of the papacy, the celibacy of priests, and the celebration of the Mass. After he was excommunicated he wrote a brilliant new German translation of the Bible. He was, by the end of his life, the main architect of the Reformation.

McCabe, Herbert 1926–2001. Great Dominican preacher and writer. Sometimes described as radical orthodox or subversive traditional. Among his best-known work is *God still matters*.

McGahern, John. Contemporary Irish writer.

McNabb, Vincent OP, 1886–1943. This great Dominican writer and preacher, although a witty man, was considered ascetic even by the members of his own order. G. K. Chesterton said of him, 'He was one of the few great men I have met in my life.'

MacNeice, (Frederick) Louis, 1907–63. Northern Irish poet and scholar.

Macaulay, Rose 1881–1958. She was a prolific novelist, broadcaster and essayist. After her correspondence with a Cowley Father, Father Johnson (published as *Letters to a Friend*) she rediscovered her Anglican faith. Her love for a married man and her long religious search became the subjects of her best-known novel, *The Towers of Trebizond*.

Mahon, Peter 1909–81. Labour MP for Preston South.

Mandelstam, Nadezhda 1899–1970. Wife of Osip who (after he was arrested) committed all his poetry to memory and then fled to the east of Russia. The two volumes of her diaries were published first in the West as *Hope against Hope*.

Mandelstam, Osip, 1891–1938. Great Russian poet who was exiled by Stalin for a poem in which he piloried the dictator, and who was eventually sent to a concentration camp in Siberia, where he died.

Maugham, W. (William) Somerset, 1874–1965. Although he wrote several very successful plays, he is best remembered for the novels *Cakes and Ale*, *Of Human Bondage*, and *The Moon and Sixpence*, and even more so for his short stories, which are among the best in the language.

Mauriac, François, 1885–1970. French novelist and journalist whose novels such as *Thérèse Desqueroux* and *Noeud de Vipères* were mainly set in the Landes near Bordeaux. Awarded the Nobel Prize for Literature in 1952.

Meredith, George, 1828–1909. English poet and novelist.

Merton, Thomas, 1915–68. Trappist monk, writer and poet. Became famous when he published the *Seven Storey Mountain* about his conversion to Catholicism and his life as a monk. Later in life he became less idealistic about monastic life, and it was not until he became a solitary living near the Kentucky monastery in a cinder hut that he became interested in most of the controversies of his time: the Cold War, death camps and the US preparations for war with Russia. He died by accidental electrocution while on a visit to Thailand.

Millay, Edna St Vincent, 1892–1943. One of the most popular American poets of her time.

Monchanin, Abbé, 1895–1957. In 1947, after working in the poor parish of St Etienne, near Lyon, he achieved his longed-for goal of setting up an Ashram in Tamil Nadu, in Southern India. He left India only to die ten years later.

Monteverde, Claudio, 1568–1643. Italian composer, and probably the father of Italian opera; amongst his famous works are *Orfeo*, and *l'Incoronazione di Popea*.

Montini, Cardinal, 1897–1978. Son of a newspaper editor, he became Pope Paul VI. He continued the work of the Second Vatican Council but reaffirmed the Church's stand on contraception *in Humanae Vitae* against much opposition.

Muggeridge, Malcolm, 1903–90. A Communist in his youth and a late convert to Catholicism, he was always a great journalist. His prophetic but unpopular account of the gulags was written when Solzhenitsyn was still a teenager.

Mumford, Lewis, 1895–1990. This great scholar, architectural critic, historian and philosopher preferred to speak of himself simply as a writer. He was a vehement critic of nuclear war and the Vietnam war, and was award the Presidential Medal of Freedom. He wrote the philosophical works *Values for Survival* and *The Myth and the Machine*.

Myers, Leopold Hamilton, 1881–1944. Wrote the great unsung masterpiece *The Root and the Flower*, of which *The Pool of Vishnu* was a part. His growing idealism was matched by despair and he killed himself in 1944.

Newby, Eric. Contemporary travel writer.

Newman, John Henry, 1801–90. Cardinal Archbishop of Westminster. There was great deal of stormy publicity when he converted from Anglo-Catholicism to Catholicism. He wrote the *Apologia* after a fierce attack by Charles Kingsley. Besides hymns and sermons, he wrote the poem *'The Dream of Gerontius'*.

O'Connor, Flannery, 1925–64. Born in Savannah, Georgia, this great Southern novelist, who said that she wrote from the standpoint of Christian Orthodoxy, was nevertheless extremely original in her writing, which also contained some of the best prose in the language. She died of the illness lupus which had kept her an uncomplaining invalid most of her short life. Her best-known works are her short stories and the novel *Wise Blood*.

Origo, Iris, 1902–88. Writer, biographer and scholar whose mother was Anglo-Irish and whose father was American. She married Marchese Antonio Origo and spent most of her life in Tuscany. Her best known books are *The Merchant of Prato* and *War in Val d'Orcia*.

Owen, Wilfred, 1893–1918. Together with Siegfried Sassoon he is one of the greatest war poets in the First World War. Died seven days before the Armistice. One of his most famous poems, 'Anthem for Doomed Youth' was incorporated into Benjamin Britten's *'War Requiem'*.

Paget, Francis, 1851–1911. Bishop of Oxford, Regius Professor of Pastoral Theology, and Canon of Christchurch, Oxford. He wrote *The Spirit of Discipline* and other sermons.

Pascal, Blaise, 1623–62. French mathematician, scientist, religious polemicist and apologist. As a scientist he invented the calculating machine. As a Christian apologist, the *Pensées* (mostly unfinished fragments) is his most famous work. It was written to try to persuade the sceptics and non-believers of his time of the necessity of religious belief. He believed also that reason alone could not discover God and that intuition, 'the heart', played a vital role.

Pasternak, Boris, 1890–1960. Studied music for six years before deciding to devote his life to literature. In Russia, famous as a poet though generally known internationally for the novel *Dr Zhivago*. Received the Nobel Prize for Literature in 1958 and was later forced to decline it.

Pelagius, ?360–?420. British theologian. His dispute with Augustine was of far-reaching importance. Though it was complicated and subtle, it can be rendered loosely: Pelagius believed that all men were free to choose good and reject evil. Augustine believed that men needed God's grace in order to use the freedom which God's grace had given them.

Perreyve, Henri, 1831–68. French orator and religious writer.

Plato, 429–347. The great Greek philosopher. He was a student and disciple of Socrates. When Socrates was executed, Plato went on to found his own philosophical school, the Academy, which occupied him for the rest of his life. His masterpiece was *The Republic*.

Plotinus, ?204–270. Born in Egypt. Neoplatonic philosopher and mystic.

Raçine, Jean, 1639–99?. Raçine was a great French playwright who started by studying philosophy but abandoned this for a busy society life. His patron was Madame de Montespan. He wrote comedies but his tragedies are his greatest works, of which *Andromaque and Phedre* is the best known outside France.

Rahner, Karl, 1904–84. Born in Breisgau, West Germany. One of the most important Catholic theologians of the twentieth century and a major influence on Vatican II. He became a Jesuit and taught at Innsbruck, Munich and Munster. One of the proposals for which he is famous is the 'anonymous Christian'. He considered that the men and women of different persuasions, including atheism, may be saved through their acceptance of the grace of Christ.

Rilke, Rainer Maria, 1875–1926. German poet born in Prague. Worked for a year as Rodin's secretary. In 1910 wrote the famous *Notebook of Malte Laurids Brigge*. Greatly admired by the philosopher Wittgenstein and poets as diverse as Stephen Spender and Pasternak.

Robb, Peter. Contemporary Australian writer.

Robertson, Frederick W., 1816–53. He was considered suspicious by the High Church of England and also the Evangelicals. His printed sermons had great influence after his death.

Robinson, F. W., 1919–83. He was a brilliant scholar who held no chair, an Anglican suffragen bishop without a diocese. Through his books, such as *Honest to God*, he reached millions of people who would not normally listen to bishops, and his social teaching was widely influential.

Rossetti, Christina Georgina, 1830–89. One of England's greatest female poets, she was a devout Protestant and rejected two offers of marriage on religious grounds. She speaks in her poetry and prose of her longing for God.

Russell, Bertrand, 1872–1970. British philosopher, mathematician and social critic. He was also one of the founders of analytical philosophy. He made important contributions to history, politics and religious studies. He won the Nobel Prize in 1950. His most famous work, written with A. N. Whitehad, was *Principia Mathematica*.

de Ruysbroek, Jan, Blessed, 1294–1381. Flemish theologian and Rhineland mystic.

Saint Exupéry, Antoine de, 1900–44. Writer, philosopher and aviator. He fell in love with flying as a child in the Drome where he went to see air shows. In the 1930s he flew small, dangerous aircraft for the first international courier service, which took the mail to Africa and South America. His great novel about North Africa was written in an outpost on the edge of the Spanish Morrocan desert. His best-known works are *Vol de Nuit* about an air raid over Arras in Northern France, and *Le Petit Prince*, a story for children. He was killed in a reconnaissance flight over southern France and his body wasn't found until 2004.

St Jerome, 331–420. Doctor of the Latin Church, together with Augustine, Gregory the Great and Ambrose of Milan. Born in Dalmatia, died in Jerusalem. A vigorous apologist, he wrote the first Latin translation of the Bible from the Greek.

St Margaret Mary Alacoque, 1647–90. Paralysed for four years as a child, she became a Visitation nun at Paray-le-Monial in Burgundy. She founded the great devotion to the heart of the suffering Christ.

Santayana, George, 1863–1952. Born in Madrid. Graduate of Harvard and taught philosophy there for twelve years. Wrote many philosophical works. Settled in Italy where he became a recluse until he died.

Sassoon, Siegfried, 1886–1967. Writer and poet. He lived as a country gentleman, hunting and writing poetry until the First World War where he won an MC, and was unsuccessfully recommended for a VC. He was critical of the war but returned to the front after being wounded. A friend of Wilfred Owen and Robert Graves, and a war poet also. His most famous prose work is *Memoirs of a Foxhunting Man*.

Sheen, Archbishop Fulton, 1895–1979. One of the best known spokesmen of the Catholic Church in the USA.

Shelley, Percy Bysshe, 1792–1822. Shelley wrote the great lyric poems

'Ode to the West Wind' and 'Adonais' in Italy, where his body was swept away in a shipwreck. Cremated in the presence of Byron, his friend, and buried in the Protestant cemetery in Rome. His second wife was Mary Godwin who wrote *Frankenstein* when she was nineteen.

Skelton, Sir John, ?1460–1529. Poet. Educated at both Oxford and Cambridge. He was tutor to Henry VIII and enjoyed the king's favour despite his outspokenness. He is said to have been imprisoned by Wolsey and he died in sanctuary.

Smith, Delia. Contemporary English cookbook writer.

Smith, Stevie (Florence) 1902–71. English writer and poet who wrote witty, often acerbic, poetry in spite of what appeared a dull life spent with her aunt in Palmers Green.

Smith, Sydney, 1771–1845. Great wit but also a humanitarian who fought against the prison system and the condition of Ireland among other ills of his time. Rector of a parish in Yorkshire and later at Combe Florey in Somerset. His outspokenness kept him from higher office in the Church of England.

Stark, Freya, 1893–1993. She mastered classical Arabic and Greek literature and this gave authority to her great travel books. The best known are *The Southern Gates of Arabia* and *The Valleys of the Assassins*. She was a natural traveller, never minded discomfort

and was besides a brilliant photographer who illustrated her own books. She lived the last years of her life in Asolo, northern Italy.

Suso, Heinrich, Blessed *c*.1300–1366. German mystic.

Sykes, Christopher, Contemporary writer and biographer.

Taylor, Jeremy, 1613–67. Imprisoned four times by the Parlementarians, he went on to become Bishop of Down and Connor. His writing is full of practical advice as well as psychological insight.

Teilhard de Chardin, Pierre, 1881–1955. Born into an old French family, Teilhard became a Jesuit, distinguished scientist of human origins, a fervent Christian mystic and a prolific religious writer. Throughout his life he reflected on the meaning of the Christian Gospels in the light of modern science, especially in relation to evolutionary theory. His great works are *Le milieu divin* and *The Phenomenon of Man*.

Teresa of Avila, 1515–82. Though she is so well-known as a mystic and visionary, Teresa was also a practical reformer who founded that branch of the Carmelite Order known as the Discalced Carmelites. These men and women wear sandals instead of shoes to indicate their poverty, discipline and the foregoing of honour. Teresa was a passionate woman of strong opinions, and her prose was fresh and energetic. She believed, above all, in uniting the will to the will of a compassionate and loving God.Her best-known works are *The Way of Perfection* and *The Interior Castle*. Doctor of the Church.

Thérèse of Lisieux, 1873–97. Lived an uneventful life in a Carmelite convent in Lisieux,which she entered by special dispensation at 15, and she died of tuberculosis at the age of 24. Nevertheless her spirituality, which is based on complete self-surrender to God's mercy and love, has inspired millions of Christians. In her *Story of A Soul* she explains her little way of perfection which consists in doing the smallest things out of love. Like her namesake she is a Doctor of the Church and a patron saint of missionaries.

Thirkell, Angela, 1890–1961. Author of more than 30 light-hearted novels of English country life.

Thompson, Francis, 1859–1907. First failed to become a priest and later three times failed his medical degree. Used opium to ward off depression and became an addict. Destitute for a time until the poet–publisher Wilfred Meynell and his wife took him under their wing. In the four years he kept off opium he wrote his most famous work *The Hound of Heaven*. Died of TB and opium poisoning.

de Tourville, Abbé Henri, 1842–1903. *Vicaire* of St Augustine's in Paris, he was forced to retire because of ill health and lived the rest of his life in retirement. During the last twenty years of his life his robust and optimistic *Letters of Direction* have given thousands of people renewed hope in the masterpiece of Divine Love.

Traherne, Thomas, 1637–74. A clergyman living in Herefordshire. His anonymous *Centuries of Meditations* and other poems were discovered on a London bookstall in 1908. His delight in childhood and the God-given beauty of the world is unique in English literature.

The Cloud of Unknowing – Written AD 500. A collection of treatises by the profound and nameless mystic who called himself Dionysius the Areopagite.

Underhill, Evelyn, 1875–1941. Baron von Hugel became her spiritual director. She helped almost single-handedly to revive twentieth century interest in mysticism, through her own work and through her translations of Hilton, Richard Rolle and *The Cloud of Unknowing*.

Updike, John. Mordant contemporary American writer.

Vaughan, Henry, 1622–95. High Church and Cavalier. Came from an ancient and distinguished family. After his conversion by George Herbert he wrote powerful religious poetry.

Voillaume, René, devoted follower of Charles de Foucauld and founder of the Little Brothers of Jesus.

Washington, Booker T., 1856–1915. Born into slavery in Virginia. Worked in the salt mines. Founded Tuskagee Institute in Alabama, the first faculty for black education in the United States. *Up from Slavery*, his autobiography, was a popular and critical success.

Watts, Isaac, 1674–1748. Non-conformist preacher and writer of 500 hymns.

Waugh, Evelyn 1903–66. Novelist. He was an assistant school master before publishing his first novel *Decline and Fall*. He travelled in Africa as a correspondent for *The Times* and as a war correspondent in Abysinnia, after which he wrote *Scoop*. He won the Hawthornden Prize for his biography of Edmund Campion, then served in the army until 1945 and won the James Tait Black Memorial prize for the trilogy *Men at Arms*. Just after the war he wrote *Brideshead Revisited*.

Weil, Simone, 1903–43. French philosopher and writer. She graduated in philosophy together with Simone de Beauvoir, and in between teaching jobs she worked in a Renault factory in order to understand the life of the workers there, and later as a farm labourer in the south of France. During the war she was called to work in London for the French Provisional Government where she wrote the famous study *The Need for Roots*. After her death her brilliant and original philosophical work was published by Gallimard, through the influence of Camus.

Whistler, Jill. Much loved wife of the poet and glass engraver Lawrence Whistler

Whitehead, Alfred North, 1861–1947. Mathematician and philosopher. Together with Bertrand Russell published *Principia Mathmatica*, the greatest single contribution to logic since Aristotle.

Wilder, Thornton, 1897–1975. Won the Pulitzer Prize for his beautifully told second novel *The Bridge of San Luis Rey*. He won another Pulitzer Prize for the play *Our Town*, and a third for *The Skin of Our Teeth*. *The Merchant of Yonkers* became another success as the musical *Hello Dolly!*

Yeats, William Butler, 1865–1939. A great poet and playwright, the son of a painter and the brother of the painter Jack Yeats. W. B. Yeats will always be associated with the Irish Revival, together with Lady Gregory and J. M. Synge: but his greatness made him a poet of the world and in T. S. Eliot's words, 'He was one of those few poets whose history is the history of their own time, and who are part of the consciousness of an age which cannot be understood without them.'

INDEX